The Transfiguration
of Christ and Creation

The Transfiguration
of Christ and Creation

JOHN GATTA

WIPF & STOCK · Eugene, Oregon

THE TRANSFIGURATION OF CHRIST AND CREATION

Wipf & Stock
An Imprint of Wipf and Stock Publishers
199 W. 8th Ave., Suite 3
Eugene, OR 97401
www.wipfandstock.com

ISBN 13: 978-1-60899-674-2

Manufactured in the U.S.A.

For Christopher Bryan and Tom Macfie,
kindred companions on the Mountain way

The seemingly infinite power for transfiguration in every region of the universe speaks of an inexhaustible fecundity at the root of reality.

—Brian Swimme and Thomas Berry, *The Universe Story*

Contents

Illustrations

Preface

THE SCRIPTURAL ACCOUNT OF Jesus' Transfiguration has for some time seized my imagination as an icon of mystical hope, beauty, and possibility. Supposing that such might also have been the case for others, or could at least become their experience, I felt moved to compose a book rather different from most of my earlier writing in a scholarly vein. Though I have long been concerned with the interplay between literature and religious faith, my previous work focused mainly on the interpretation of American literary texts and cultural history. I now wanted to write a book more explicitly theological, yet also more subjectively colored and broadly encompassing, than what I had attempted thus far. But I would like to think that my lifelong engagement both with matters of faith and with imaginative literature can usefully inform an endeavor of this sort. So it has been natural for me to include here a fair number of literary examples, but without supposing that readers of this book will necessarily have had prior familiarity with all the texts I cite.

Despite renewed academic interest in the Transfiguration, as evidenced by publications that have appeared in recent years, this emblem of universal transformation remains comparatively obscure. My treatment, unlike most others, highlights post-biblical expressions and environmental implications of the Transfiguration mystery. Compared with many previous commentaries, my approach is less strictly concerned with visual iconography in the Eastern church, more broadly attentive to East-West connections and to aesthetic windows to the divine opened through literature and music. Cosmological consequences of the Transfiguration, though they have been noted elsewhere, are a central theme of my inquiry. In the pages that follow, I particularly hope to address readers who are concerned to advance the present-day search for fresh yet biblically grounded approaches to "green theology." In this last sense, the book continues an engagement with issues I explored in an earlier volume, *Making Nature Sacred: Literature, Religion, and Environment from the Puritans to the Present.*

Scholarship ordinarily means building upon, and benefiting from, the labors of those who have gone before. That has certainly been the case for me in writing this book, and I am particularly grateful in this regard to two authors I have never met: John Anthony McGuckin, whose masterful compilation of patristic and other primary source documents in *The Transfiguration of Christ in Scripture and Tradition* proved invaluable to me, and Andreas Andreopoulos, whose study of relevant themes in Byzantine theology and iconography has also taught me much.

My first attempt to articulate through an oral presentation to others, several years ago, what amounts to the germ of this book's argument I owe to an invitation offered me by the Rev. J. Robert Wright of General Theological Seminary, so I am grateful for that early opportunity. Throughout this project and others that preceded it, my astrophysicist friend, Arnold Benz, has remained an unfailing source of sympathy and intellectual stimulation.

I am grateful as well for the friendship, inspiration relevant to this project, and profound Christian fellowship I enjoyed through my extended association with a group of inquiring souls that met at Hie Hill near Westbrook, Connecticut, and came to be called the Transfiguration Community. Members of that group whose personal influence meant most to me include Olive Brose, the late Richard Brose, Carole Brown, David Brown, Joy Coolidge, and Ted Coolidge.

In the process of completing this book following my move to Sewanee, Tennessee, in the fall of 2004, I have likewise benefited in diverse ways from coming to know many persons in this vibrant community who have enriched my life, thought, and spiritual development. Several of them have contributed more specifically to my understanding of ecotheology or other issues addressed in the book. Such kindred spirits include former student Corey French; Robin Gottfried, director of Sewanee's nascent Center for Religion and Environment; Jennifer Michael; Henry Parsley, Episcopal Bishop of Alabama and former University Chancellor; Bran Potter; Bill Stafford; and Tom Ward. Librarian Jim Dunkly has been, as always, helpful in supplying bibliographic leads; and Kathy Hamman provided valuable editorial and technical assistance.

Sewanee's university and village community, situated on upland of the Cumberland Plateau, is often referred to as the Mountain. So I was intrigued to find that Sewanee's distinguished theologian William Porcher DuBose had once been inspired, in a sermon of his delivered at a 1911 reunion held in his honor, to compare this feature of local topography to the biblical mount of Transfiguration. Discussed in conjunction with topics I address in chapter 8, this discourse can also be found reprinted in the Appendix.

For permission to reprint here in altered form portions of an article that first appeared in the *Sewanee Theological Review*, I am indebted to the journal's editor, Christopher Bryan. But as the Dedication of this book should indicate, I am grateful to Christopher, biblical theologian par excellence and cherished friend, for a great deal more than this. I am likewise indebted to my canoeing buddy, university chaplain Tom Macfie, for his never-failing discernment, good cheer, and good humor. Finally, I am once again and as always grateful to my wife, Julia, not only for advice on the manuscript but for a lifetime of sharing with me her sustaining love together with her rare theological and critical acumen.

Introduction

The Transfiguration as Verbal Icon

THE IMAGE OF JESUS transfigured with light on "a high mountain" beside Moses and Elijah stands apart as a luminous yet baffling point in Christianity's gospel narratives. It seems anomalous at first by comparison with other accounts of Jesus' ministry in Galilee, since it offers neither parable nor saying, healing miracle nor episode of encounter with the crowds. Presented in all three synoptic gospels, this strangely visionary moment stands at once within and outside ordinary time.

Though the calendar recognizes "the Transfiguration of Our Lord" as a notable feast day, celebrated on August 6 in several church communions as well as in lections for the Last Sunday of Epiphany, the occasion draws little attention from Christians in the Western Church. Many in today's secular world have never heard of it. Yet the Transfiguration of Jesus, which looks at first like a gratuitous interlude in the gospel narrative, emerges as the focal point of all Creation when viewed in the light of contemplative traditions both ancient and modern. It is an image that draws us to envision the coalescence of humanity and divinity, time and eternity, Passion and Resurrection, God and Creation.

As such, the Transfiguration or "metamorphosis" (Mark and Matthew characterize the event with the expression *metamorphōthē*) constitutes a great mystery of faith. It presents us with an icon of final transformation already outlined on the face of mortal limitation. It verifies our hope for the eventual renewal of all things. And it challenges us, by way of transformed vision, to behold divine beauty at the heart of creation.

In writing this book, I wanted to explore what the multilayered gospel story of Jesus' Transfiguration might mean for us today. Toward that end, I also hoped to recover an appreciation of how it has been variously interpreted by writers, visual artists, musicians, liturgists, and theologians over the centuries. What does the Transfiguration disclose not only about Jesus, but also about the prospect of seeing our human nature transformed? What does it tell us about how the entire cosmos stands transfigured in the light of Christ? How might this vision of New Creation shape the earth-centered spirituality that has begun to surface lately in response to our planet's ecological crisis? And given that August 6 also marks the date of nuclear cataclysm at Hiroshima, how can we reconcile the vision of a transfigured cosmos with all that life and history show us of disfigurement, death, and affliction?

Such are the concerns I have been drawn to pursue in a book that blends historical inquiry and literary analysis with more personal meditation on the Transfiguration's significance for our time. While benefiting from the detailed commentaries available for each of the three variant gospel versions, I wanted to reflect mainly on the story as a whole. I do not purport to offer a full, chronologically ordered survey of how attitudes toward this subject evolved from the apostolic era through successive centuries. I do not pursue certain technical problems of exegesis—whether, for example, the "high mountain" should be identified with Mount Tabor or with Mount Hermon, or whether the episode's telling has been transposed from memory of a post-resurrection appearance. Biblical scholars have addressed such matters elsewhere.[1] Nor do I propose a factual explanation of how the Transfiguration story originated. At this late date, we cannot hope to know the actual, experiential circumstances underlying the evangelists' poetic account of a mountain climb in Galilee. Who can presume to say what literally took place on that extraordinary day when Jesus, accompanied by three apostles, is said to have reached the summit of a remote peak where he suddenly becomes luminescent while conversing with Moses and Elijah? Bishop Kenneth Stevenson, reflecting on his own experience of climbing hills with friends, plausibly raises "the possibility that Jesus and his 'inner cabinet' went on a long trek, perhaps on more than one occasion, and that these special times apart, the climbing up and down included, made a significant impact on their sense of vocation and destiny."[2] In any event, it is clear enough that the episode, as related in Mark, Matthew, and Luke, draws many biblical ideas and references into one vibrant image.

The Transfiguration thus represents a visualization through words of realities both seen and unseen. The biblical account is best appreci-

---

1. Such commentary typically highlights distinctive features of each gospel account in separate chapters. A recent and useful example is Lee's *Transfiguration*.

2. Stevenson, *Rooted in Detachment*, 131.

ated, therefore, not as simple narrative but as a verbal icon depicting a numinous moment. For the gospel writers, this icon of the Word centers and reflects Jesus as the Christ, the ultimate icon of God. Pictured here, as in the mystically charged renditions by Saint Paul and the author of John's gospel,[3] is a cosmic Christ rather than the historically confined Jesus of Nazareth. Despite the small space this scene occupies within the biblical text, it fills a huge tableau of signification. The panentheistic vision[4] of its poetry-in-prose shows the light of a triune God irradiating all creation, offering thereby an arresting scriptural illustration of the ultimate icon. Not surprisingly, then, Eastern Orthodox iconographers have often been drawn to render this scene in their art.

In Eastern Orthodox iconography, liturgy, and theology, the Transfiguration has enjoyed special prominence. Its feast day was celebrated in the East by the latter part of the fourth century and widely established there long before its official sanction as universal for the Western church by Rome in 1456.[5] It may be no accident that Francis of Assisi, as a favorite Latin saint, is said to have borne bodily witness to the stigmatic marks of crucifixion, whereas the body of Saint Seraphim of Sarov, a popular Orthodox model of sanctity, is remembered instead as having displayed the radiance of Transfiguration. Nonetheless, the Western Church has also sustained a lesser-known tradition of reflecting creatively on the Transfiguration event. Apart from Raphael's famous painting (see fig. 1), this tradition has typically expressed itself not so

---

3. This gospel, alone among the four, includes no account of the Transfiguration. By general consensus, this omission is best explained by recognizing that the image of a glorified Christ is so all-suffusing in John that it requires no separate attention or description. This gospel, as the last to be composed, might also suppose on the part of its readers prior knowledge of some episodes, including the Transfiguration, that had already been amply represented in all three synoptic gospels.

4. As distinguished from pantheism, which regards the universe itself as divine and disavows notions of a personal God, panentheism sees the created order infused with God's presence while its creator remains transcendent, distinguishable from creation.

5. For an overview of how traditions of exegetical understanding about the Transfiguration developed through the patristic era, together with a useful collection of translated primary sources from the Greek and Latin Fathers, see McGuckin, *The Transfiguration*. Other notable commentaries include Heil, *The Transfiguration of Jesus*; Lossky, *The Mystical Theology*; Nes, *The Uncreated Light*; and Andreopoulos, *Metamorphosis*. The opening chapter of Williams' *The Dwelling of the Light* features devotional remarks on the spirituality of transfiguration iconography. There have been at least some signs lately of renewed interest in the Transfiguration's significance for our time. Such interest is evidenced, for example, by the publication of books such as Dear's *Transfiguration*, Tutu's *God Has a Dream*, and Stevenson's *Rooted in Detachment*.

much visually as verbally, in writings from several genres produced by literary artists and church leaders as well as theologians. Dante, Thomas Traherne, William Porcher DuBose, T. S. Eliot, Edwin Muir, Pierre Teilhard de Chardin, Evelyn Underhill, Michael Ramsey, Annie Dillard, and Desmond Tutu—these discerning souls are among the "cloud of witnesses" in Western Christianity whose imaginations have been stirred by reflection on the Transfiguration. The list includes a few musicians, too, such as Olivier Messiaen, the twentieth-century French composer of *La Transfiguration de Notre Seigneur Jésus-Christ* (1965–69) for chorus and orchestra. Among modern theologians of the Western Church, I have found Pierre Teilhard de Chardin, Michael Ramsey, Jürgen Moltmann, and Desmond Tutu particularly helpful in endeavoring to fathom the mystery of Transfiguration.

Figure 1

Back in 1949, Michael Ramsey urged in a groundbreaking essay that while the Western Church had been slow to recognize the Transfiguration, its theology had "special significance for the present time."[6] Archbishop Ramsey's statement still rings true, particularly as applied to the present-day search for fresh, yet biblically grounded approaches to ecotheology. To a surprising degree, exegetical discussion of Christianity's relation to environmental ethics and practice has been confined within a narrow band of Old Testament texts. In fact, the scriptural site of this debate rarely extends beyond the creation stories and "dominion over the earth" language clustered in those first two chapters of Genesis! Even fewer New Testament passages have attracted serious reflection on the topic.

This constricted field of biblical reference is typically presumed in arguments set forth not only by those who blame Jewish and Christian teaching for sponsoring exploitative attitudes toward the nonhuman world, but also by some who extol the environmental teachings they take to be implicit in biblical Christianity. Clearly, there is a pressing need to identify new biblical points of reference for a contemporary spirituality and theology of creation. The Transfiguration offers just such a model. It qualifies as "new," of course, not as a freshly invented novelty but as a recovery of truths which, as Henry Thoreau once put it, "were never old." The paradigm of Transfiguration encourages us to view creation as a continuously evolving transformation of matter and energy, a dynamic immediacy, rather than a one-time leap from nothingness situated in the distant past. As Teilhard de Chardin so clearly perceived, such a dynamic cosmology requires a theology for our post-Darwinian era that is responsive to the spirit of evolutionary science. Transfiguration also highlights Christ's role in the New Creation, thereby leading us to identify the process of creation not simply with a time of origins, but with God's ideal and future fulfillment of redemption. So Transfiguration carries the promise of extending our horizon of faith—beyond belief in the world's original goodness, toward a vision of eschatological hope.

In addition to its ecumenical links with Eastern Orthodoxy, then, the Transfiguration presents the Western Church with a rich spiritual source for confronting environmental issues and pursuing that larger "integrity of creation" that has come to be discussed in forums like the World Council of Churches. Proponents of the international Earth

6. Ramsey, *The Glory of God*, 5.

Charter (2000) have likewise urged cultivation of "a new reverence for life." But while the Church's official response to environmental issues is often dominated by moralisms linked to a worthy but insufficient theology of stewardship, I believe that what Ramsey has called "the gospel of Transfiguration" holds power to inspire reverential awe before the wonder and beauty of God's Creation. The Transfiguration points symbolically toward a doxological (from the Latin *doxa*, with reference to divine glory) rather than a resource-management model of apprehending our relation to the natural world. I argue, in fact, that Christian churches would do well to celebrate a common Day of Transfiguration to serve as a religious counterpart and complement to Earth Day, the secular environmental festival celebrated on April 22 in the United States.

One way to begin unfolding the many-layered meaning of the Transfiguration is to approach its richness sequentially, through a three-stage progression of themes. The first and most obvious stage of meditation addresses Christ's illumination, in which the earthly Jesus of Nazareth is shown to be transfigured into a unique bearer of divine glory. So my treatment begins on this plane, with a close reading of the relevant gospel narratives in conjunction with other biblical texts. The second stage of reflection involves recognition of how our human nature is transfigured in Christ. Here I recall the ways in which both literary artists and theologians have envisioned humanity's elevation and transformation in the larger light of Transfiguration. The final stage of reflection expands to consider how a cosmic Christ also illuminates the nonhuman, material order of being. This last dimension, weighing the consequences of a Transfiguration gospel for the whole of Creation, has been explored both poetically and, more discursively, by Eastern Orthodox theologians such as Sergei Bulgakov. It also bears the most direct connection to environmental spirituality.

This threefold pattern of reflection—from Christ transfigured to a transfigured humanity and cosmos—is traced sequentially through each of the three opening chapters. This sequence resembles, in fact, the course of a meditative exercise. The theme of environmental theology and spirituality, first sounded in chapter 3, is recapitulated in the final chapter. Other chapters in Part Two of the book consider the spiritual, aesthetic, social, and ethical *consequences or ramifications* of a Transfiguration gospel, with the benefit of understanding derived from both Eastern and Western traditions. Père Teilhard, for example, in his

1923 prose poem called "Mass on the World," dramatizes the Eucharistic aspect of Transfiguration and Christ's interfusion with the whole material cosmos.

Although my inquiry centers inevitably on Christian traditions of theology and spirituality, the larger significance of the Transfiguration would seem to be anything but esoteric or narrowly sectarian. Meditating on this image can influence profoundly our views of God, our own human nature, and the nature of the cosmos or divine milieu we inhabit. One might say, in fact, that the Feast of the Transfiguration deserves to be more universally known because it images that point of coalescence where just about everything comes together. It epitomizes that rare occasion in our sadly bifurcated world when we can glimpse the luminous conjunction between sacred and profane, time and eternity, human and divine, Creator and Creation. Its biblical presentation fuses word with visual image. Recovering access to the gospel of Transfiguration must, I would suppose, advance the ecumenical project of rapprochement between Eastern and Western traditions of Christian spirituality. And as I hope to indicate along the way, broader ideals of human and cosmic metamorphosis have likewise been honored as central in a variety of religious traditions other than those tied to biblical Christianity.

Finally, then, the Transfiguration deserves meditative scrutiny precisely *because* its iconic presence in Scripture transcends critical analysis. And its spiritual significance, as I hope the following pages confirm, draws us beyond moralism toward a mystical imagination that is similarly evoked in many great works of art. No wonder Russian Orthodox theologian Bulgakov called it "the feast of beauty." For Teilhard de Chardin, "the most beautiful mystery" of the Transfiguration likewise symbolized "all that I believe and love."[7] Thomas Merton has suggested that institutional religion, without losing its prophetic address to social needs and realities, needs to recover its mystical character to retain relevance in the contemporary world. Beauty, too, is a value that I believe humanity today hungers to reclaim, even if it is unmentioned or disdained in many sectors of our postmodern consumer culture. So beauty, poetry, hope, and a contemplative rootedness in elemental Being—all of these and more the Transfiguration signifies, which is why this mystery so fully merits our attention.

7. Bulgakov, "The Exceeding Glory," 191. Teilhard's remarks (my translation) are cited in Siehen's article on the Transfiguration in *Dictionnaire*, 15.394.

PART I

Three Aspects of Transfiguration

1

Icon of the Invisible God

THE BIBLICAL ACCOUNT OF how Jesus' appearance came to be transfigured with glory on a mountain in Galilee holds a striking place in the synoptic gospel stories. Though evidently written out of the faith-community's experience of the Risen Lord, it suggests more than a simple foreshadowing of the Resurrection—or, as interpreted by some commentators, the endtime glory of the Second Coming. In Mark's elemental version, the episode follows logically and closely ("six days later") from Jesus' self-disclosing dialogue with Peter at Caesarea Phillipi.[1] After reaching this summit of the Galilean ministry, Jesus descends—first to heal a boy troubled by an unclean spirit and then southward to death in Jerusalem. Yet Mark, whose gospel otherwise highlights the bizarre, "anomalous frightful" character of events surrounding Jesus' ministry and passion, also dramatizes the sheer terror that seizes three disciples at the Transfiguration.[2] They are quite overwhelmed and undone. So unsettled are they from commonplace reality that their encounter with the numinous takes place in a visionary moment, standing at once within and outside of historical time. Jesus himself, according to Matthew, calls the incident a "vision" (*horama*, 17:9), a term that in this context would mean something closer to authentic seeing than to phantasm.[3] Together with Peter, James, and John, we as readers are arrested by a moment of truth, in which our normally opaque world suddenly becomes diaphanous.

Despite its arresting character, then, the Transfiguration shows affinities with several genres of biblical literature. It contains elements

1. Bryan, *A Preface to Mark*, 99–102.
2. Geyer, *Fear, Anomaly, and Uncertainty*, 19–63.
3. Lee, *Transfiguration*, 41.

of apocalyptic writing, of post-resurrection testimonies, and of New Testament epiphany scenes (including Jesus' baptism), by virtue of which it dramatizes yet another manifestation of Jesus' distinct messianic identity. Following the precedent set by Old Testament narratives, this revelation of Jesus as Light can also be recognized immediately as a theophany, or earthly appearance of divinity:

> Six days later, Jesus took with him Peter and James and John, and led them up a high mountain apart, by themselves. And he was transfigured before them, and his clothes became dazzling white, such as no one on earth could bleach them. And there appeared to them Elijah with Moses, who were talking with Jesus. Then Peter said to Jesus, "Rabbi, it is good for us to be here; let us make three dwellings, one for you, one for Moses, and one for Elijah." He did not know what to say, for they were terrified. Then a cloud overshadowed them, and from the cloud there came a voice, "This is my Son, the Beloved; listen to him!" Suddenly when they looked around, they saw no one with them any more, but only Jesus. As they were coming down the mountain, he ordered them to tell no one about what they had seen, until after the Son of Man had risen from the dead. (Mark 9:2–9)

As the icon paintings make plain, this particular disclosure of divine glory takes a decidedly tripartite shape, with its primary triptych of Moses, Jesus, and Elijah paralleled by the second triptych of disciples Peter, James, and John. Another threefold pattern discernible here is a vital interaction among the Father's authoritative voice, the Son's appearance as enlightened flesh, and the Holy Spirit's overshadowing presence in the cloud. Greek Fathers of the church, including Origen and Andrew of Crete, developed Trinitarian interpretations of the pattern. And the Venerable Bede affirmed "that when the Lord was baptized in Jordan, so on the mountain, covered in brightness, the whole mystery of the Holy Trinity is declared."[4]

Within and beyond this multiform texture, though, one is struck by the singular and central positioning of Jesus in the scene. Traditional iconography reinforces that impression. Jesus stands between the two great prophets of Hebrew faith and expectation. One way of understanding his placement here is to see him poised historically between Moses, through whom the Torah became mediated from the ancient past, and Elijah, the herald of Israel's consummated future at the end of time. Or, Moses and Elijah might be seen in interpretations like that of John

---

4. McGuckin, The Transfiguration of Christ, 113–14.

Chrysostom as typifying respectively a duality of Law and Prophets, dead and living. In any event, Jesus stands at the circle's center, the point of crossing between timelessness and time. (See fig. 2, p. 6)

It is not only along the horizontal plane of this scene that Jesus upholds the center. Along the vertical axis as well, Jesus on the "high mountain" (whether identified as Tabor or Hermon) stands *between* earth and heaven, on a fracture point of the *axis mundi* where he mediates the energies flowing between God and the world. Likewise within the narrative span of the evangelist's temporal portrayal, this transfigured Jesus stands at or near the center of things. In Mark's version, for instance, the episode in question comes just after the eighth of sixteen chapters. At this midpoint and turning point of the gospel narratives, from a high place in Galilee, Jesus is about to descend to death in Jerusalem. Just before he is to be disfigured by the dark brutality of the passion, he is transfigured by the light of glory. In Luke's version (9:28–36), the theophany is immediately preceded by Jesus' warning of his approaching demise in Jerusalem, a "departure" or "exodus" about which Luke believes that Moses and Elijah can be overhead speaking on the Mount. All three evangelists insert reminders of Jesus' suffering and death just after telling of his illumination. And no sooner has Jesus made his way down from the heights than the gospels portray him as confronted with the misery of a convulsive child.

The Transfiguration is thus a glory bounded by affliction. Framing it on one side are the past words and deeds of Jesus' Galilean ministry; on the other, the specter of his future degradation. The Transfigured Christ not only contains the whole of history, collapsing linear time into a timeless moment, but encompasses as well the full emotive span of individual experience. And we can see this dramatic coalescence reflected visually in the mandorla and circular blocking of traditional Orthodox icons (as illustrated, for example, in the Novgorod icon, figure 2).

Figure 2

As an instance of the numinous, the Transfiguration gospel narratives convey that peculiar blend of fear and attraction characteristically associated with experiences of the sacred. The disciples are evidently awestruck—and startled directly from slumber in Luke. Yet they are also touched, uplifted, even zealous (in the case of Peter) to memorialize the occasion by leaving three booths or tabernacles on the site. Matthew specifies that these abject witnesses are "touched" quite literally by Jesus, who also urges them to "Get up" and "not be afraid" (Matt 17:17). Their sense of superlative wonder at seeing Jesus clothed in divine luminosity is suggested in Mark through the mention of garments whiter than anyone on earth could bleach. In Matthew and Luke, the disciples behold something of the brilliant source of life and light in Jesus' face, which shines "like the sun" and thus invokes the typology of Moses' transformed visage in the Book of Exodus. Later tradition, particularly in the Orthodox East, would ponder at some length the mystical meaning of this uncreated, all-suffusing light. Both Mark and Matthew emphasize, too, the unsettling abruptness of the apparition, which comes and goes "suddenly" and without warning.

All three synoptic writers suggest the vanity of building commemorative booths when Jesus himself is the ultimate tent or tabernacle or place of meeting between God and humankind. Peter is presumably right so far as his confiding to Jesus that "Rabbi, it is good for us to be here" (Mark 9:5). If anything, "good" (or beautiful, *kalon*) is an understatement. Peter, James, and John enjoy the singular privilege of entering an immense concentration of sacred space and time on the mount, which has instantaneously become a new "Beth-el," or dwelling place of God. And this indwelling presence, as confirmed by John's gospel and the whole body of New Testament teaching, is here to stay. But Peter cannot resist the impulse to grasp the sacred moment. "Let us make three dwellings," he proposes, "one for you, one for Moses, and one for Elijah." It is indeed fitting to link these great prophets to the leafy branches used in the Jewish Sukkot festival, and we shall eventually want to consider some implications of that suggestion for "green" religion. Peter seems misguided, though, to presume that fulfilling the promise of Transfiguration depends somehow on his own initiative.

One suspects that had Peter enjoyed access to modern camera equipment, he would have rushed to record this occasion visually, trying to capture the moment but failing thereby to let the moment take possession of *him*. As usual, Jesus' disciples—even those in the favored inner circle—don't quite get the point. Mark tells us outright that Peter spoke without "knowing what to say." Even though awed silence best suits an encounter with the Absolute, nervousness often makes us want to say *something*—almost anything—when facing an overwhelming experience. Understandably, Peter wants to capture, prolong, and honor this startling incandescence that he witnesses but cannot understand.

We can identify readily enough with Peter's urge to domesticate lightning,[5] to tame this colossal energy within some form of human fabrication. Yet God, in order to be God, must remain wild, uncontainable. The mountain is itself a reminder of God's creation beyond the usual scope of human use, habitation, or control. And though Jesus stands on the mountain, he inhabits nothing less than the whole earth—indeed, the whole cosmos. The author-farmer Wendell Berry has aptly declared that God "is the wildest being in existence."[6]

It seems altogether fitting that Jesus had, according to Luke, sought this mountain solitude in order to pray. So it is while praying, while enacting the deepest possible communion with the Father, that his own divine nature manifests itself. If prayer entails communication beyond the usual coordinates of space and time, it is also appropriate that Jesus should be talking directly here with Moses and Elijah. The three disciples, too, are drawn—willingly or not—into that fierce energy field of Jesus' prayer. And as frequently happens when people pray, they end up getting not only more than they expected, but more than they may have thought they wanted. The Jesus the disciples thought they knew becomes strangely Other and thus, for a moment, slightly scary.

In sum, the synoptic Transfiguration story presents Jesus as the ultimate icon of God. This inference coincides with the declaration of Colossians 1:15 that "he is the image (*eikon*) of the invisible God." As such, the Jesus icon at once discloses divinity through a human face *and* suggests paradoxically that elusive essence, that transcendent mystery still preserved behind a cloud of unknowing.

---

5. Psalm 77:18 (with its reference to God's lightnings that "lit up the world") supports the traditional exegetical link—invoked in Eastern Orthodox liturgy, as well as in the Latin Introit for August 6—between natural lightning and the burst of illumination on Mount Tabor.

6. Berry, "Christianity," 101. Lewis, in *The Lion*, makes a comparable point when his characters observe that Aslan is "'not like a *tame* lion.'" 182.

Above all, as ultimate icon, Jesus provides a visible and vocal "likeness" of God, a restored image of the divinity in humankind. All other icons serve merely as copies of this one, images of the Christological image. To behold this image is likewise to intuit its unseen depths. The synoptic vision of Jesus on the mount becomes a lens, as it were, through which one catches a view of the world's restoration. With their gaze concentrated on this focal point of history and a transfigured cosmos, the disciples in Matthew's version end up seeing "no one"—and, I'd presume, no thing—"but only Jesus." "Only Jesus" becomes all in all.

The disciples, then, are privileged to see their familiar rabbi in a new light. Yet the narratives certify that they fail to comprehend what they have seen. Neither is it clear that the event provokes any permanent change in their view of the world. In fact, readers of the gospel texts, especially latter-day readers gifted with the perspective of a long church tradition, are in some ways privileged to "see" more in the evangelists' verbal icons of the event than first-century witnesses ever could. As readers and as members of what literary critics might now call an interpretive community, we envision the Transfiguration vicariously through the eyes of Peter, James, and John, but from another angle of perception. And our view of the Jesus icon is necessarily mediated through the evangelists' word-drawings.

Like the visual icon, a text that functions as verbal icon requires us to look *through* the surface, to behold the dynamic source *behind* the individual words or brushstrokes. This beholding is a meditative act, drawing forth impulses of emotion and will beneath the plane of rational cognition. The iconic medium of the written Transfiguration narratives embraces, in turn, several forms of verbalization, including the voice from the cloud, reference to Jesus' discourse with Moses and Elijah, and Peter's dialogue with Jesus. Through this range of discourse, the Word re-presents itself from the text to later generations of readers and potential witnesses.

What the Transfiguration gospel thus conveys to us about Jesus, beyond his previously unforeseen power and majesty, is the all-surpassing beauty of his presence. So it is indeed "good for us to be here," in a world hallowed materially by virtue of its infusion with the Lord's body. The evangelists' visionary portrayal of Jesus' metamorphosed face and clothes is precisely that—a vision. Far from a journalistic report, it defies our literal understanding. As a visionary expression of religious truth, it is nonetheless real and true. Thus, the Transfiguration epitomizes not only the beauty of holiness, but also the holiness of beauty as represented to us through art and imagination.

Gregory Wolfe, drawing in turn on theologian Hans Urs von Balthasar, has aptly proposed that the Transfiguration has much to tell us about a "spiritual aesthetic," linking Scripture with that which nature and human art likewise reveal about God. Wolfe's remarks on this theme are revealing:

> Of all the passages in the Bible that relate to beauty as a window onto the divine, the most neglected, and most important, is the story known as the Transfiguration. On the surface, nothing about this episode speaks directly about art, beauty, or the imagination. But placed in the right context, one can see in this passage a spiritual aesthetic. . . .
>
> According to von Balthasar, the essential starting point for the human encounter with the divine is a moment of aesthetic perception, that glimpse of radiance, mystery, and meaning we see in a work of art or in the natural world. In the context of von Balthasar's theology, the seemingly straightforward story of the Transfiguration takes on new twists. . . .
>
> Thomas Aquinas defined beauty as the splendor of form, the flash of radiance that is at once intensely pleasurable and filled with meaning. In the Transfiguration, the burning light that once appeared to Moses in the bush now pulses from Jesus himself, revealing him as the God-man, the icon of the Father. Beauty and meaning embrace. . . .
>
> At its best, art transfigures the world around us for a brief time, strives to let the radiance of truth, goodness, and beauty flash out for an instant. Art wakes us up, trains our perceptions, and reminds us that when we try to build rigid structures around presence we inevitably lose what we attempt to keep. The purpose of art is not to strand us in an alternate world, but to return us to the realm of the ordinary, only with new eyes.[7]

It should not surprise us, then, to find the Transfiguration's fuller meaning opened to us not only through the exegesis of theologians, but also through the imaginative creations of verbal, visual, and musical artists. For surely the truths embodied in art, including the art of Jesus' own parables, are no less real than those reported as simple fact. Michael Ramsey points out that the episode has long maintained a mystical ap-

---

7. Wolfe, "Editorial Statement: Transfiguration," 3–4.

peal for Eastern Christians because it came to be treated in that tradition less as "an event amongst other events and a dogma amongst other dogmas than a symbol of something which pervades all dogma and all worship."[8] As an integrative symbol, it speaks not only to the intellect but to the deep psyche, where the most profound religious truth always resides. It irradiates not only a Galilean mountaintop, but the eye of the heart. This visionary episode is the very epitome of what it would mean to "see" the wholeness of all things illumined at once by art, nature, and scriptural revelation.

8. Ramsey, *The Glory of God*, 137.

2

And we shall all be changed

W E HAVE CONSIDERED THUS far how the vision of Jesus glorified on the mount recalls the divine encounters of Moses and other Old Testament prophets. It also anticipates the future glory to be revealed at the Lord's Resurrection and Second Coming. Yet it signifies still more. The Transfiguration amounts to more than a symbolic foreshadowing and more than a gospel reiteration of Jesus' divine Sonship, as had already been supplied at his baptism. A second dimension of the Transfiguration mystery involves a crucial recognition of how our *human nature* has been renewed and elevated in the person of Christ glorified.

Eastern Christianity has always been unusually attentive to the goal of "deification" or *theōsis*, our participation in God's own life by sharing in Christ's union of divine and human natures. And the Church—particularly the Eastern Church—has commonly read the Transfiguration episode as a dramatization of *theōsis*. "We were with him on the holy mountain," writes the author of 2 Peter, assuming the voice of Peter as eyewitness. Yet if we read the collective pronoun here expansively enough, it includes all of us who stand "with him" there in gospel fellowship, thereby discovering a solidarity more intimate and profound than simple proximity of place.

So while the synoptic accounts do not dwell explicitly on the transfiguration of humanity, other scriptural texts help to establish this point. Thus, Paul writes that "all of us, with unveiled faced, seeing the glory of the Lord as though reflected in a mirror, are being transformed into the same image from one degree of glory to another" (2 Cor 3:18). The iconographic principle of reflection operative here amounts to this: we are apt to *become* that which we gaze upon at length. For as Paul concludes, "it is the God who said, 'Let light shine out of darkness,' who has shone in our hearts to give the light of the knowledge of the glory of God in the face of Jesus Christ" (2 Cor 4:6). Moreover, Luke's report that Jesus ascended the mountain in order to pray seems to confirm humanity's yearning for inner transformation.

When we say with the evangelists that Jesus is transfigured on the mountain, we needn't suppose, after all, that it is *he* who undergoes substantive change or metamorphosis. Perhaps Jesus did himself attain some definitive realization or mystical illumination at this juncture, as he inwardly assimilated his future passion and glorification. Evelyn Underhill makes an appealing case for this theory.[1] Yet Luke's descriptive qualification, "the appearance of his face changed" (9:29), offers ground for another interpretation with longstanding support in Christian tradition. In this second view, the mountaintop experience did not alter Jesus so much as the disciples' perception of him.

In his book, *The Mystical Theology of the Eastern Church*, theologian Vladimir Lossky concurs that from the standpoint of Eastern Orthodoxy, Jesus as the Christ of God underwent no essential change in his Transfiguration. What changed instead was the awareness of the disciples, who now witnessed the supernal, uncreated light in which he lived. It is doubtful, in view of subsequent events, whether these witnesses were able to assimilate and to preserve full comprehension of what they had seen. But for the moment, at least, their impression of Jesus—rather than Jesus himself—had decidedly changed. By way of confirmation, Lossky cites a homily of Saint Gregory Palamas: "The light of our Lord's Transfiguration had neither beginning nor end; it remained unbounded in time and space and imperceptible to the senses, although seen by bodily eyes . . . but by a change in their senses, the Lord's disciples passed from the flesh to the Spirit."[2]

This stress on the inner change of witnesses accords with the Pauline formulation in 2 Cor 3:18, whereby "all of us . . . are being transformed"—undergoing, that is, some kind of inner metamorphosis. Such was the change attributed to Saint Seraphim of Sarov, in whose eyes and countenance his interviewer perceived a dazzling radiance that produced in turn a transfigurative effect on others.[3]

---

1. Underhill, *The Mystic Way*, 120–31.
2. Lossky, *The Mystical Theology*, 223–24.
3. Gorainov, *The Message of Saint Seraphim*; Zander, *St. Seraphim of Sarov*.

Indeed, the Transfiguration episode enables us to see something of ourselves contained in God. Writings from both Western and Eastern church traditions illustrate this theme. Thus, Orthodox liturgical texts for Transfiguration vespers affirm that "today Christ on Mount Tabor has changed the darkened nature of Adam, and filling it with brightness He has made it godlike." Accordingly, we share in Christ "the glory and splendour" of God.[4]

In Western literary tradition, Dante's rendering of the spiritual ascent toward perfected vision in *The Divine Comedy* offers a vibrant illustration of how Transfiguration bears on *theōsis*. While ascending from earth at noon of the vernal equinox, the pilgrim-narrator in the opening canto of *Paradise* undergoes an inward transformation when he gazes at his beloved Beatrice who, in turn, reflects the radiance of the sun. He finds himself momentarily elevated (Italian *trasumanar*) above his normal human nature. Then by the 23rd canto, when he reaches the eighth heaven of the fixed stars, he is able to behold the divine substance of Christ streaming forth its radiance amid the Church Triumphant, much as it had on the mount of Transfiguration. By the time he reaches the realm of pure light, the empyrean, he sees not only the beauty of Beatrice transfigured beyond human telling, but also the universe itself, all substances and accidents, enfolded into one.

At the climactic height, when the pilgrim undergoes his last change of vision to see God configured in the shape of a Tricolored Sphere, he is startled to find reflected therein an image of humanity. His shock of recognition comes from seeing iconically *through and into* the illumined sphere, from discovering his own humanity conjoined with eternal perfection in an image of exalted *anthropos*. The beatific vision presents our own human image glowing with godliness, embraced within the Trinity itself. In this way Dante dramatizes the vision of humanity's transfiguration in Christ:

> But my sight by seeing learned to see,
> The transformation which in me took place
> Transformed the single changeless form for me. . . .
>
> The sphering thus begot, [the Son] perceptible
> In Thee like mirrored light, now to my view—
> When I had looked on it a little while—

---

4. *The Festal Menaion*, 469, 477.

Seemed in itself, and in its own self-hue,
Limned with our image; for which cause mine eyes
Were altogether drawn and held thereto.[5]

To see thus in Jesus' Transfiguration the potential and restored glory of human nature is, admittedly, to find a meaning beyond what the gospels explicitly declare. Yet as Michael Ramsey and others have observed, such second-level conclusions began to be drawn at an early stage of church history, in patristic writings by Latin and Greek Fathers, including Jerome, Augustine, and Leo the Great as well as Origen and Basil. A comparably exalted view of human potential is likewise represented in the familiar patristic aphorism, attributed to Clement of Alexandria, that the Logos became human so that humans might aspire to become divine.

In any case, the gospel writers' language of transfigurative metamorphosis suggests something more than a cosmetic alteration of appearances. To be sure, the metamorphosis of humanity envisioned here involves a restoration of the divine image within us, a return to what we were always meant to be, rather than a full-scale remaking of our nature—but it amounts to a *change* nonetheless. So the idea of a transformed humanity is directly allied with the classic scriptural theme of conversion or *metanoia*. Particularly during the Reformation era, many in the Western Church urgently wished to understand what it meant to undergo a process of personal conversion. How, they wondered, might people prepare themselves—or predispose others—to receive the grace of conversion? Does conversion simply turn us in a different direction, or does it make us new people indeed? To what extent does regenerative conversion demand the extinction of one's old identity? And what further understanding, we must now ask, might a gospel of Transfiguration contribute to this ancient question about change of heart?

Part of what the Transfiguration suggests about conversion, I think, is that God wills to make us new, to enlarge our capacity for glory, without destroying the uniqueness of our old personality. Our original human nature is to be fulfilled, not annihilated, even though we know ourselves to be inherently flawed, sinful, and downright quirky creatures. By the same token, God on the holy mountain recasts all the old materials into a new creation, freshly illumined from within.

5. Alighieri, *The Comedy: Paradise*, 346.

This metamorphosis therefore renews our humanity without destroying it. One reason why Jesus on the mountain appears curiously alien to the disciples is that they have yet to know the ultimate, glorified identity of their resurrected Lord. Even after the Resurrection, as in Luke's poignant story of two disciples who walk beside Jesus on the road to Emmaus, the risen Christ remains at first unrecognizable (24:13–27).

At another level, though, such dramatizations of Jesus' divine strangeness confront us all the more intensely with the mystery of our own humanity. Existentially, we sometimes find ourselves to be strangers to ourselves, to say nothing of other human beings. Literary productions by Hawthorne, Poe, Dostoevsky, and other great writers witness abundantly to this truth. When I look back at old snapshots of myself in high school, for example, I feel a bemused pity toward the insecure, bumbling adolescent who stares back at me from those photos. And I barely recognize myself at all in infant photos. To affirm the continuity of one's being across several decades of memory and change requires a kind of faith.

Saint Paul insists that the process of human transformation continues even beyond the bounds of this mortal life. For he is given to understand that, through the mystery of the general resurrection, "We will not all die, but we will all be changed, in a moment, in the twinkling of an eye, at the last trumpet." And just as the disciples witnessed on the mountain a change in Jesus' bodily character, so also Paul envisions this ultimate "change" in our humanity as a holistic transformation, in which "this perishable body puts on imperishability," and "this mortal body puts on immortality" (1 Cor 15:51–54).

Yet within the course of our lives, though we may imagine that we welcome change in ourselves, we often find real metamorphosis to be painful. Such is birth, such is death, such is our struggle to begin new phases of life, especially following the death of our hopes or of our loved ones. While faith, according to Saint Paul, offers grounds for hope that "our inner nature is being renewed day by day" (2 Cor 4:16), he believes that such renewal is commonly driven by affliction. So it is hardly coincidental, I think, that Dostoevsky adopted as the epigraph for *The Brothers Karamazov*, his most intense dramatization of human nature and its search for God, Jesus' sober reminder of what transformation must finally entail: "Very truly, I tell you, unless a grain of wheat falls into the earth and dies, it remains just a single grain; but if it dies, it bears much fruit" (John 12:24).

We can find solace, though, in pondering more expansive implications of the natural, botanical figure that supports this saying—as remarks by Parker Palmer from another context help to disclose:

> Transformation is difficult, so it is good to know that there is comfort as well as challenge in the metaphor of life as a cycle of seasons. Illumined by that image, we see that we are not alone in the universe. We are participants in a vast communion of being, and if we open ourselves to its guidance, we can learn anew how to live in this great and gracious community of truth. We can, and we must—if we want our sciences to be humane, our institutions to be sustaining, our healing to be deep, our lives to be true.[6]

Inevitably, though, any progress we make, under grace, toward realizing our truest and best selves falls short of our goal. However long my list of New Year's resolutions, I know I am largely stuck with *who I am*, to the extent that my genes, training, and circumstances have already defined me. Conversion must therefore work through, rather than despite, the obstinate individuality that defines who I am as a unique personality. Thus, Saint Paul, aware of his peculiar defects, insists that he "will boast all the more gladly of my weaknesses, so that the power of Christ may dwell in me," since Paul understands that "power is made perfect in weakness" (2 Cor 12: 9). The grace of Transfiguration finally enlarges us toward involvement with something and someone beyond our petty desires—but also, paradoxically, reduces us to our original, essential being before God. This reductive process of conversion may require a painful stripping away of egoism, the loss of familiar comforts. So it is a counterpart of the *kenosis*, the self-emptying humility that Jesus embodied through his incarnation and death on the cross. The self's radical reduction opens a way for God, who enters the emptiness to transfigure it. Buddhist tradition likewise speaks of encountering *sunyata*, a void or emptiness bearing the potential for self-renewal.

Such a divine transformation through absence can be seen, for example, in the testimony of Gonville ffrench-Beytagh, Dean of St. Mary's Cathedral in Johannesburg, before he was charged with anti-apartheid subversion of the South African state and placed in solitary confinement. Beyond the other indignities of life in prison, he was deprived of

---

6. Palmer, *Let Your Life Speak*, 97–98.

all usual means for celebrating the Eucharist. But ffrench-Beytagh re-
cited the communion liturgy anyway, as best he could remember it. And
he soon felt himself gathered, as never before, with the whole company
of heaven. He had no bread or wine. So as he approached the words
of consecration, he simply embraced the absence of his condition. The
result was a startling instance of illumination, transfiguring his prison
cell into the gate of heaven:

> I took nothing in my hands and I said, "This is my body, which is
> given for you. Do this in remembrance of me." And again I took
> nothing in my hands and I said, "This is the blood of the new
> testament which is shed for you and for many, for the remission
> of sins. Do this as often as you shall drink it in remembrance of
> me." And I'll tell you this, against all my whole teaching—as a
> bigoted Anglo-Catholic I suppose—it is my honest knowledge
> that the communions that I received in that prison cell, without
> the means of bread and wine, were as real and as glorious and
> as triumphant and as magnificent as any communion I've ever
> received in my own cathedral, with the organ going and the in-
> cense and the bells and all the glory. Just as real and wholly as
> healing and as complete. That is my witness and my evidence.[7]

Edward Bouverie Pusey, noteworthy Oxford professor and a leader
of the nineteenth-century Tractarian (Anglo-Catholic) movement in
the Church of England, also understood the divinizing potential of the
Transfiguration in sacramental terms. Like the metamorphosis enacted
through the Eucharistic elements, Christ's transformation on the mountain witnessed for Pusey to "that ineffable mystery, how man can be
taken into God, how God can dwell in man, and fill him with the glory
of the Father." Or, as Pusey summed up the matter, "His Transfiguration
is our glory."[8]

Often, though, the godly image imprinted on humanity is obscured
from view by the tedium of daily life, as well as by sin and weakness of
imagination. Often, too, the godliness of our birthright has been overshadowed in the Western Church by preoccupation with humankind's
fallen or depraved condition. Still, even writers schooled in Calvinist
tradition have been moved to envision humanity's participation in
divine glory. For example, this vision of *theōsis* suffuses the poetry of
Edward Taylor, a seventeenth-century Puritan minister who served the

---

7. ffrench-Beytagh, *Tree of Glory*, 76.
8. Bouverie Pusey, "Sermon 87," 227, 238.

with nothing less than transformative union with God. Not only Jesus' favored disciples, but also contemplatives of later ages might hope to achieve this union. Such a mystical experience likewise transformed the way a soul perceived its physical surroundings, or as Symeon affirmed: "You, the light, are joined to the grass in a union without confusion, and the grass becomes light; it is transfigured yet unchanged."[7] Defending the devotional practices linked to *hesychia*, an inward stillness attained through repetitive prayer, Palamas argued that the uncreated light shining from Christ on Mount Tabor reflected God's energies, as distinct from God's essence. Though at base ineffable and nonsensory, this illumination might occasionally be received—and even channeled through bodily eyes—by human beings.

Gregory's distinction between essence and energy reflects an impulse to preserve that familiar theological paradox of a God who is at once transcendent and immanent within the created world. Thus he understands the Christian deity as "both being and non-being . . . everywhere and nowhere . . . everything and nothing."[8] It is worth considering how this central paradox, which applies as well to descriptions of the incarnate and visible yet quite supernal light of Transfiguration, happens to resemble the way modern physics describes the essential nature of light. Is electromagnetic radiation best understood in terms of waves or particles? Paradoxically, both views seem plausible. Even after Newton's corpuscular theory was discredited, Einstein's photon hypothesis confirmed the notion of energized particles without material mass. Current theory holds that photons share this oddly ambiguous status with other force particles, such as gluons and gravitons. In fact, scientists have lately been concluding that "*all* matter has a wavelike character."[9]

As Christian thought developed beyond the apostolic period, the crucial paradox of a Creator's transcendent, yet intimately enfleshed relation to Creation found apt expression in the doctrine of the Holy Trinity. Trinitarian spirituality has crucial importance not only for later readings of the Transfiguration, but also for present-day Christian efforts to encourage the "greening" of religion. Particularly during the last century, monotheism has often been charged with undermining ethical imperatives toward environmental reform. *If* one sees God as the su-

7. Ware, "Eastern Christendom," 148.

8. Ibid., 151.

9. Greene, *The Elegant Universe*, 104.

isolated frontier community of Westfield, Massachusetts. Taylor's poetic meditations, which remained unpublished until the modern era, dramatize his amazement at finding his human nature raised to rapturous union with the divine. Taylor perceived that by virtue of God's incarnation in a human being, humanity had been raised higher than the angels and had even been seated—through the God-Man Christ—within the Holy Trinity. Poem after poem of his rhapsodizes on the wonder of discovering this transfigurative glory. In a poem titled "The Experience," Taylor relates the marvel of finding himself enwrapped by a supernal "Beam of Light" that discloses to him, in the course of his celebrating the Eucharist, "My Nature with thy Nature all Divine / Together joyn'd in Him that Thou, and I." His ecstasy leads him to declare, with witty boldness:

> I'le Claim my Right: Give place, ye Angells Bright.
> Ye further from the Godhead stande than I.
> My Nature is your Lord; and doth Unite
> Better than Yours unto the Deity.[9]

In "The Transfiguration," a twentieth-century poem that Scottish writer Edwin Muir composed from the standpoint of Jesus' disciples, the speaker testifies to sensing that day a renewal that is physically palpable. The radiance emanating from Jesus renders the disciples "whole," with hands suddenly "made new to handle holy things" and "the Source of all our seeing rinsed and cleansed." Momentarily, at least, the experience takes them out of themselves and gives back to them "the clear unfallen world." The light from Jesus' clothing, like a blessed contagion, affects their garments as well:

> We would have thrown our clothes away for lightness,
> But that even they, though sour and travel stained,
> Seemed, like our flesh, made of immortal substance,
> And the soiled flax and wool lay light upon us
> Like friendly wonders, flower and flock entwined
> As in a morning field. Was it a vision?
> Or did we see that day the unseeable
> One glory of the everlasting world
> Perpetually at work, though never seen
> Since Eden locked the gate that's everywhere
> And nowhere?

9. Stanford, *The Poems*, 9. See also Gatta, "Little Lower than God," 361–68. It is telling that Jonathan Edwards, colonial New England's best known Calvinist theologian, also preached a sermon specifically devoted to the Transfiguration.

For Muir, the glimpse of *theōsis* dramatized here remains ephemeral. Presently the glory fades. Awareness of our wounded condition returns, as the world rolls "back into its place, and we are here, / And all that radiant kingdom lies forlorn, / As if it had never stirred." Still, these disciples will always recollect that day when "The world we saw . . . made this unreal."[10] For them, as well as for us, this past experience mystically defines the future.

Looking beyond ourselves to see other human beings transfigured in the light of godliness can be more challenging, though—especially when we feel alienated from those we take to be uncomfortably unlike ourselves, from those whose actions distress us, or from those we know so well that their faults seem intolerable. How, amid such darkness, can the divine light of Transfiguration be seen? A celebrated passage in Thomas Merton suggests that for him, as for Jesus' disciples on the mountain, the vision comes as unexpected grace. This Trappist monk may have been predisposed toward such discovery, after spending years in prayer and interior reflection. But he neither predicted it nor produced it. Tempted for a time to look down on those pursuing mundane lives in the "world" outside the precinct of monasticism, Merton describes a singular moment in which he sees a glowing nimbus surrounding the people he observes in the streets of downtown Louisville:

> In Louisville, at the corner of Fourth and Walnut, in the center of the shopping district, I was suddenly overwhelmed with the realization that I loved all those people, that they were mine and I theirs, that we could not be alien to one another even though we were total strangers. It was like waking from a dream of separateness, of spurious self-isolation in a special world, the world of renunciation and supposed holiness . . . I have the immense joy of being man, a member of a race in which God Himself became incarnate. As if the sorrows and stupidities of the human condition could overwhelm me, now I realize what we all are. And if only everybody could realize this! But it cannot be explained. There is no way of telling people that they are all walking around shining like the sun.[11]

Still, there is no better way of describing what a transfigured humanity might look like than to say that people are "all walking around

10. Muir, "The Transfiguration," 174–75.

11. Merton, *Conjectures*, 156–57.

shining like the sun." And such words aptly reflect the tradition by which Saint Seraphim of Sarov, the great nineteenth-century Russian *staretz*, gained renown as one whose inward transformation toward likeness to God shone forth physically in the dazzling brightness of his countenance. Seraphim, whose own spirituality was closely linked to the Feast of Christ's Transfiguration, taught that such light surrounded other people as well, though it typically remained unseen, as though projected through another wavelength of electromagnetic radiation. Thus Motovilov, a beloved disciple, expressed fright at beholding Seraphim's blinding brightness:

> Then Father Seraphim gripped me firmly by the shoulders and said: "My friend, both of us, at this moment are in the Holy Spirit, you and I. Why won't you look at me?"
>
> "I can't look at you, Father, because the light flashing from your eyes and face is brighter than the sun, and I'm dazzled!"
>
> "Don't be afraid, friend of God, you yourself are shining just like I am; you too are now in the fullness of the grace of the Holy Spirit, otherwise you wouldn't be able to see me as you do."[12]

Like Merton, then, Seraphim developed a capacity to discern the Transfiguration's interactive relevance to humanity at large. For that matter, latter-day evolutionary theory suggests an even broader vision of what Transfiguration is all about. The divine interfusion of matter and energy dramatized in the scriptural icon of Transfiguration applies well beyond the human animal to other forms of life. Today it seems increasingly clear that nonhuman creatures, too, must reflect something of the divine image and possess their own mysterious quality of "soul." Animals can no longer be discounted—in the manner Descartes once believed—as mere mechanisms. They, too, share the sacred breath of life and are gifted with capacities beyond our understanding.

Such has long been the belief of archaic peoples, as well as of certain select figures in Christian tradition—including the eighteenth-century American naturalist William Bartram and Quaker reformer John Woolman. To affirm the special glory of human nature and consciousness should not oblige us, either as Christians or as human beings, to belittle the interiority of all other animals by contrast. Although present-day genetic science proves nothing about God as such, it can contribute powerfully to our imagining the unseen continuity of all life. As Carolyn

12. Zander, *St. Seraphim*, 90.

Servid reminds us, the alphabet of life is composed of just four "letters" paired across the double spiral of the DNA molecule. Despite the immense variety of species and individuals expressed in genetic code, "the sixty-four words in the DNA cells of all of those species—plant and animal alike—are precisely the same sixty-four words," so that "all living things on earth are linked by a common language." This "holy connection" strikes Servid most poignantly as she thinks about the genetic bond that links her own physical being to the composition of a thrush whose death she watches one day in Alaska.[13]

Nor does our kinship with the rest of creation stop there. We know that the elemental essence of our bodies is nothing more—or less—than stardust. The very stuff of our life and breath—starting from carbon, oxygen, hydrogen, and nitrogen atoms together with the energy that animates us—all derive from cosmic processes set in motion some 14 billion years ago at the time of the Big Bang. Astrophysicist Arnold Benz describes in graphic terms just how closely our human constitution is bound to the evolutionary history of the universe:

> The carbon and oxygen in our bodies stem from the helium combustion zone of an old star. Two silicon nuclei, merged in the early phase of a supernova explosion, become the iron in our blood's hemoglobin. The calcium in our teeth formed during a supernova out of oxygen and silicon. The fluoride with which we brush our teeth was produced in a rare neutrino interaction with neon. The iodine in our thyroid glands arose through neutron capture at the onset of a supernova. We are connected directly with the development of stars and are ourselves part of the cosmic history.[14]

It is at once sobering and exhilarating to consider thus where we came from. And yet, modern science belies the image of a straightforward linear cosmology traceable to one instant of origins. Instead, as Benz shows, cosmic history unfolds as a continuous creation—an endlessly dynamic and innovative course of incremental developments. This evolutionary cosmogenesis seems to me quite consonant with the spirituality represented in the biblical scene of Jesus' Transfiguration. As Jesus is transfigured, his physical matter becomes a diaphanous extension of light-energy. Jesus, the disciples, and even the mountain's physi-

13. Servid, "The Right Place," 222–23, 228.
14. Benz, The Future, 32–33.

cal mass spill over their boundaries of discretely defined autonomy to embody a common process of "new creation." Ultimately fulfilled in the Resurrection, this re-creative process ties the irradiated humanity of the disciples not only to God but also to the divinely illumined earth of the mountain.

Benz, in a fascinating sequence that he calls "An Astronomical Breathing Meditation," points out that with each deep inhalation a person's lungs take in about one liter of air containing an immense number of molecules in motion—about three-quarters of them nitrogen, most of the rest oxygen. He concludes that some of these same molecules must have been present at the time of Jesus.[15] So it is fascinating to imagine what we share, materially as well as spiritually, with those three soul-brethren whose breath quickened with amazement on the mountain. The Transfiguration event stands thus as the very epitome of transformation-within-continuity.

15. Ibid., 66.

3

Transfiguring the Material World

To move, then, toward the third and last stage of interpretation is to find the Transfiguration narratives envisioning nothing less than the future or potential metamorphosis of the cosmos in the light of Christ. Starting from the transfiguration of self, we are led to reflect on the globally expansive theme of a transformed society and on how God's grandeur might transfigure our perception of the natural world. Granted, this extension of vision requires a look beyond the primary sense of the Gospel narratives. The Transfiguration of Creation comes to light only over time, with the benefit of commentary supplied by post-apostolic tradition. And it has figured less prominently in Western liturgies than in Byzantine rites. Then again, we may not *expect* to find much sense of reverence for the wider creation to arise immediately from a festival day which, though probably first celebrated around Jerusalem from the fourth or fifth century,[1] was ordered into general Western observance by Pope Callixtus III in the mid-fifteenth century to celebrate a military victory over the Turks.

But in the realm of imaginative art, poets and other writers in the West *have* for some centuries been fashioning verbal icons of a transfigured creation. Representing such a spiritual metamorphosis of perception has been central to the expression of writers such as Thomas Traherne in the seventeenth century, the English Romantic poets (albeit commonly in more secular terms) in the nineteenth century, and many later writers.

---

1. Thus, Kenneth Stevenson explains that one earlier reason for settling on August 6 would have been to fix a date forty days before Holy Cross Day (September 14), on the supposition that the Transfiguration took place forty days before Jesus' crucifixion. See Stevenson, *Rooted in Detachment*, 13.

At least two features in the biblical story have particularly stirred later writers and theologians to understand the Transfiguration as an icon of transformation applicable not only to human nature but also to the whole of creation. One such element is the rugged mountain setting. The story's isolated peak, which figures prominently in most painted icons, draws our vision immediately beyond human-centered civilization toward an untamed, nonhuman world. In images such as the Novgorod icon, portrayal of the slope's jagged topography underscores its remoteness from the more linear or symmetrical shapes produced by human culture.

In this regard, one can scarcely forget how often high summits have figured as preferred sites of encounter with the numinous throughout the Hebrew Bible. The momentous scenes of God's revelation to Moses at Sinai or Horeb come most readily to mind. According to 1 Kings 19:8, Horeb—"the mount of God"—likewise provides the setting for Elijah's theophany in sounds of silence. So Moses and Elijah, the two great prophets flanking Jesus in the transfiguration triptych, evidently have special warrant to stand with him on high. By the same token, Solomon's Temple in Jerusalem was constructed on the sacred hill of Mount Zion, a site linked thereafter to the messianic fulfillment of Israel and the healing convergence of all nations. The mount of Transfiguration is but one of the several prominences highlighted in Matthew's gospel, which concludes with Jesus' mountain commission to "make disciples of all nations" (28:19). Yet the Hebrew Bible repeatedly shows how mountain settings bring the human subject closer not only to heaven, but also to threatening powers of wind, storm, and lightning. Such displays of un-contained, unpredictable force suggest, in turn, the unbounded, largely unseen might of a Creator who is capable of animating creation with wild abandon.

Remnants of a primordial sense, according to which sacred power emanates directly *from* the mountain, can be discerned in several portions of the Hebrew text. Hence God's ancient title of El Shaddai, with its overtones of frightening force, preserves tribal memories of localized mountain and storm deities whose veneration preceded recognition of the universal Lord. Greco-Roman mythology similarly situated the abode of Zeus and other immortals on Mount Olympus, and pre-Columbian native peoples in the American Northwest had long revered the snow-capped peak of Mount Rainier, otherwise known as Tacoma.

Denise Levertov, an Anglo-American poet who spent her last years in Seattle, wrote a moving series of poetic meditations on the brooding presence and apparently numinous grandeur of Mount Rainier.[2] In "The Transfiguration," Edwin Muir's poem composed from the standpoint of Jesus' disciples, the speaker imagines metamorphosis emerging first as a kind of earth tremor directly "from the ground," while "we felt that virtue branch / Through all our veins till we were whole."[3]

The mount of Transfiguration in Galilee, though for the gospel writers removed from human settlement, is exposed as a point of close encounter between Creator and creation. Although the Lord remains wholly "other," God now inhabits and visibly suffuses the earth. God has assumed, and thereby glorified, a physical body. Patristic and later commentaries frequently underscore the fleshly, physical, bodily character of God's self-revelation on the holy mount. Christ transfigured is a transcendent—but scarcely ethereal—presence. John of Damascus, in his eighth-century remarks on the Transfiguration, observed how different was that theophany, whereby "of old on Mount Sinai, violent storms, smoke and terrifying fire veiled his great condescension, proclaiming there was no approach to the Law-Giver, the one who had only revealed his back and by his works showed that he was the supreme artificer." "But now," insists John, "everything is light and splendour for he who is the Lord and Maker of all things, himself comes forth from the bosom of the Father."[4] By virtue of the Incarnation, God became not only human but material, allied to the physical world. As one modern commentator affirms, "the whole cosmos" is "encompassed by God's union with matter," so that the Transfiguration thus reveals, among other things, "the cosmological consequences of the Incarnation."[5]

From the patristic era onward, traditional commentators have also remarked persistently on the mysterious light emanating from Jesus' countenance on Mount Tabor. Typically they describe this radiance as flowing from within Jesus' body rather than from without, as a blaze comparable to lightning in its sudden brevity. It enlightens thereby not just the face (in Luke's and Matthew's version) and garments of Jesus,

---

2. I have previously discussed these poems in Gatta, *Making Nature Sacred*, 239–43.

3. Muir, *Collected Poems*, 173.

4. McGuckin, *The Transfiguration of Christ*, 209.

5. Nes, *The Uncreated Light*, 43–44, 53.

but the fuller expanse of earth's atmosphere. So the accent on light is another feature of the scene that extends Transfiguration's meaning into the whole order of natural creation.

John of Damascus explains that "Glory did not come to this body from without," in the manner of common illumination, but "from within" to confirm Jesus' hypostatic union with the divine source of all things. Such glory is "cause for rejoicing for the whole creation." Augustine, drawing on the gospel injunction (Matt 5:14–16) to kindle a lamp to illumine all in the house, likewise affirms that in the light of Jesus' transfiguration, "The whole world is this household." Gregory Nazianzen recalls that this same divine light appeared to Moses from the burning bush and "blazed out upon Paul" in his conversion. Since indeed "God is light," God's dissemination of light is the first act of creation. Gregory observes that primordial light, "the first of all visible creation to be called into being," continues to radiate "through all the universe, the wheeling orbit of the stars and all the beacon fires of the heavens." Sharing with the Father this glory of cosmic creation, as Saint Paul confirms in Colossians 1:15, the divine Logos revealed on the mount emanates a radiance that, according to Ambrose Autpertus, effectually illumines "all things which shine with light, even the sun and moon and stars." So this unbounded light signifies at once the source of life and the consummate end of cosmological history when, as Hilary of Poitiers already finds displayed in the Transfiguration, God shall be "all in all." Moreover, when Gregory Nazianzen writes that Jesus "flashed like lightning on the mountain and became brighter than the sun, intimating mysteries of the age to come,"[6] his remark calls to mind a motif and psalm reference commonly invoked in liturgies for the feast of Transfiguration. For the psalmist, God's presence swept far across the visible landscape: "your lightnings lit up the world; the earth trembled and shook" (Ps 77:18).

Yet, for Byzantine mystical theologians, the status of that light emanating from Jesus provoked intense debate throughout the later Middle Ages. Was it simply a brilliant concentration of naturally created light, conveyed to the disciples through ordinary sense impressions? Or was it essentially uncreated, spiritually nonmaterial, and thus received through an "inner eye" of mystical perception? Symeon the New Theologian (late tenth century) and Gregory Palamas (fourteenth century) favored the latter conclusion. For Symeon, to receive this light was to be gifted

6. McGuckin, *The Transfiguration*, 207–8, 279, 170, 299, 260, 171.

premely monarchical "other" who is decidedly detached from creation, one might indeed regard nature as a dis-spirited commodity ripe for exploitation. Historically, the environmental policies and practices favored by nominally Christian cultures have too often supported such suspicions.

So is religious support for an ecological ethic better supplied by belief-systems—animistic, polytheistic, or pantheistic—that unmistakably imagine spirit interfusing with matter? Not necessarily, I think. It is one thing to affirm, from the earth-rooted Christian standpoint of Gerard Manley Hopkins, that the world is charged with God's grandeur. It is quite another to suppose that God is nothing other than the sum total of features, mass, and energy contained in the material cosmos. From the standpoint of crude pantheism, we are bound to worship every fact of nature—including the AIDS virus, the law of gravity, and every last quark—on something close to equal footing.

By contrast, the ecological merit of a Trinitarian vision lies in its capacity to mediate in dynamic fashion between the transcendence enforced by strict monotheism and the spiritual indwelling favored by pantheism or polytheism. Jürgen Moltmann explains how this point lends distinctive value to a trinitarian Christian understanding of panentheism, in contrast with pantheism. He also explains how the theology of a triune God qualifies the limitations of absolute monotheism:

> If we cease to understand God monotheistically as the one, absolute subject, but instead see him in a Trinitarian sense as the unity of the Father, the Son and the Spirit, we can then no longer, either, conceive his relationship to the world he has created as a one-sided relationship of domination. We are bound to understand it as an intricate relationship of community—many-layered, many faceted and at many levels. . . . The Trinitarian concept of creation binds together God's transcendence and immanence. The one-sided stress on God's transcendence in relation to the world led to deism, as with Newton. The one-sided stress on God's immanence in the world led to pantheism, as with Spinoza. The Trinitarian concept of creation integrates the elements of truth in monotheism and pantheism. In the panentheistic view, God, having created the world, also dwells in it, and conversely the world which he has created exists in him. This is a concept which can really only be thought and described in Trinitarian terms.[10]

10. Moltmann, *God in Creation*, 2, 98.

From the time of Origen in the second century, church theologians commenting on the Transfiguration have frequently underscored its trinitarian texture. Complementing the obvious appearance of the divine Son and the sound of the Father's voice, the presence of the Holy Spirit was often located in the cloud that overshadowed Jesus' disciples. Alternatively, all three persons of the Godhead might be identified with the overshadowing cloud or, as in the case of Palamas, with the mystical light.

The threefold patterns represented in traditional icon paintings provoke further reflection on how Trinitarian faith might construe God's relation to the world. Typically, the three disciples are portrayed in symmetrical conjunction with the three glorified figures of Moses, Elijah, and Jesus. Whereas Moses, Elijah, and Jesus seem to stand or float mostly *above* the mountain, as though already elevated to heaven, the three disciples are shown to be emphatically earthbound. They sprawl, lie, or kneel on the earth slope, their bodies often thrown cheek by jowl with rocks, trees, and low-lying vegetation. But while Jesus invariably appears on the heights above them, he is also tied visually to them and more or less directly to the mountain mass as well. Matthew's gospel emphasizes Jesus' continued bodily involvement in the creaturely world through the detail of his physical touch. After the disciples were driven to the ground, "overcome by fear," their Lord "came and touched them, saying 'Get up and do not be afraid'" (Matt 17:6–7). Jesus takes the rare initiative of touching the fearful disciples not for the sake of healing or symbolic demonstration, but simply to reassure them.[11]

Some iconographers show three rays of light running from the heavenly to the earthly trinity of persons. This visual line of connection appears, for example, in figure 2. In any case, the two triads evidently accord with each other, amid a dynamic atmosphere of light and movement, as though all six figures were engaged in an odd form of dance. It is, in effect, *the* great cosmic dance. Christian theology has traditionally understood the Trinity as encompassing a mysteriously dynamic, unceasing process of interaction among a community of divine "persons." This process, imaged especially in the Eastern Church as a kind of dance, or *perichoresis*, ends up representing not only the Trinity's internal character, but also its interactive relation to creation. So the human community and the larger community of creation are both mirrored by that

---

11. Lee, *Transfiguration*, 58.

love process perpetually enacted within the Godhead. All of this can be seen in images of the Transfiguration that discerning icon painters have produced. It is, once again, a vision consonant with the pulsating sense of creation emphasized by twenty-first century science. Subatomic physics, with its swirl of almost ineffable particles, enacts a ceaseless dance, as do vast processions of stars and galaxies. String theory suggests that at the very core of matter, each loop particle "contains a vibrating, oscillating, dancing filament." Photon "gas" flows around us so pervasively that the world would glow perpetually, as in Transfiguration icons, if our eyes could register microwave radiation.[12]

Literary imagination opens other windows onto the ecological or cosmic meaning of Transfiguration. In this respect, the vision of the seventeenth-century priest and writer Thomas Traherne, reflected in his *Centuries of Meditations*, continues to give startling witness. Traherne saw natural icons of transfiguration in a water puddle, a grain of sand, and other commonplace splendors of earth and sky. "We need nothing but open eyes," he wrote, "to be ravished like the Cherubims," to see the world as a divine temple and "the visible porch or gate of eternity." The way in which we behold our surroundings shapes much of what we see, "for the World is both a Paradise and a Prison to different persons." Traherne expresses the delight he felt as a young Anglican rector coming "into the country" of Credinhill, where he found himself "seated among silent trees, and meads, and hills."[13]

To be sure, Traherne rarely comments on the specific occasion of the Transfiguration, which was not observed as a feast day in the church of his time. Still, in the *Centuries* he dwells momentarily on the "disfigured countenance" of him who was "transfigured upon Mount Tabor."[14] A .M. Allchin tells how Traherne, in another manuscript book of meditations centered on the church year, illustrates the idea of jointly sanctified time and space with reference to the Transfiguration: "If such a memorable Action as our Savior's Transfiguration upon Mount Tabor, shall make it even by S. Peter himself to be called in the New Testament THE HOLY MOUNT, may well such Memorable and Divine Occurrences as the Resurrection of our Savior, and the Giving of the Holy Ghost make

---

12. Greene, *The Elegant Universe*, 14, 348–49.

13. Traherne, *Centuries*, 18, 57, 17, 134. While most editions of this collection are titled *Centuries of Meditations*, some are titled *Centuries*.

14. Ibid., 45.

the Times wherein they came to pass both called and esteemed HOLY TIMES. Since Times as well as Places are capable of the impression of HOLY THINGS."[15]

Beyond such passing references, however, Traherne's writing is suffused with transfigurative awareness that it is "good to be here" amid the common wonders of life on this planet. "Your enjoyment of the world is never right," Traherne insists in *Centuries*, "till every morning you awake in Heaven; see yourself in your Father's Palace; and look upon the skies, the earth, and the air as Celestial Joys."[16]

Traherne intones sensory versions of this ecstatic mantra again and again throughout his meditations. "You never enjoy the world aright," he chants, "till the Sea itself floweth in your veins, till you are clothed with the heavens, and crowned with the stars: and perceive yourself to be the sole heir of the whole world, and more than so, because men are in it who are every one sole heirs as well as you." Or again he asks, "How then can we contemn the world, which we are born to enjoy?" For "this visible World," regarded through eyes of faith, is nothing less than "the body of God." As such, it is "wonderfully to be delighted in, and highly to be esteemed." It is "a pomegranate indeed, which God hath put into man's heart."[17]

Such an ecstatic faith could not have come easily to Traherne. The son of a shoemaker and orphaned at an early age in Herefordshire, he endured the tumult of the English Civil War as a child. He was already dead at 37, leaving his *Centuries* manuscript unfinished. But his writing confirms his vision of a transfigured felicity, to be embraced here and now by anyone willing to love the visible world as part of God's own body. In contrast with the world-denying forms of asceticism that have often been recommended through the course of Christian history, Traherne's outlook is refreshing. It suggests that enjoying the world is not merely permissible but something of a Christian obligation. That is startling "good news" indeed! For as Traherne puts it, God's laws "command you to love all that is good, and when you see well, you enjoy what you love." And to see the world as transfigured rather than simply fallen is to recognize that it is already a blessed paradise, "a mirror of infinite

15. Allchin, "The Sacrifice," 27.

16. Traherne, *Centuries*, 14.

17. Ibid., 14, 5, 65, 103.

beauty," and "the Gate of Heaven." So it is even "more to man since he is fallen than it was before."[18]

Traherne's insistence on enjoying the world's beauty flowed from a robust spirituality far removed from self-centered hedonism. As A. M. Allchin and others have recognized, Traherne's vision of a transfigured creation reflects his sacramental understanding of Christ incarnate throughout the whole material body of nature.[19] Nor should Traherne's sense of the world be discounted as naively optimistic. Without ignoring affliction, his transfigurative vision looks through and beyond it.

Traherne's writing can scarcely be expected to comment directly on contemporary ecological concerns. Yet the spirituality articulated in his meditations and poems offers much that is currently applicable. Environmental reform frequently finds its motivation, after all, in some sort of earth love, including attachment to particular places and creatures. As the twentieth-century American conservationist Aldo Leopold argued in his formulation of a "land ethic," the extension of human ethics toward concern for the nonhuman world requires an expansion of vision, because we "can be ethical only in relation to something we can see, understand, feel, understand, love, or otherwise have faith in."[20] Accordingly, we feel a passion to preserve in our tangible world only that which we have learned to love. Or again, as Traherne declares, "when you see well, you enjoy what you love"—and only then will you feel an imperative to preserve it. Every page of the *Centuries* exposes the holy materialism of this author's love for creatures and grateful enjoyment of the physical world. As a result, Traherne's meditations, with their capacity to inspire renewed reverence for creation, remain a valuable source of ecospiritual wisdom.

Plainly, Traherne's sensuous delight in nature was rooted in his devotion to a particular place, in his attachment to the hilly green country of his native Herefordshire, bordering on Wales. It so happens that a comparable scene of rounded, verdant elevation appears at Mount Tabor, the site in Galilee to which tradition assigned the Transfiguration begin-

---

18. Ibid., 10, 15.

19. Allchin, *The World Is a Wedding*, 80–93, together with Canon Allchin's other remarks about the transfiguration of the world, 20, 39, 136–37; Dowell, *Enjoying the World*.

20. Leopold, *A Sand County Almanac*, 251.

ning at least as early as the third century.[21] Belden Lane, in his book *The Solace of Fierce Landscapes*, contrasts the gentle, flowering, and conical slope of Tabor with the more austere, arid, and lean shape of Sinai. He recalls that the Spanish nun Egeria visited both sacred mountains during her fourth-century travels through the Holy Land. During his own pilgrimage to Tabor, Lane is struck by the mountain's gentle beauty and profusion of vegetative growth. Through the light rain of an early spring, he notices songbirds and white-flowering almond trees. And he observes that a seventh-century Armenian pilgrim named Elisaeus had likewise been impressed by the lush appeal of Tabor. Elisaeus's account, with its sensuous response to discrete features of landscape, illustrates why Mount Tabor is indeed an appropriate vantage point for envisioning the divine transfiguration of creation:

> Concerning the beauty of the mountain and the delightfulness of the spot, if you wish to lend a willing ear I shall briefly describe the appearance of the charming place. Around it are springing wells of water and many densely planted trees, which blossom from the rain of the clouds and produce all kinds of sweet fruits and delightful scents; there are also vines which give wine worthy for kings to drink. . . . The path by which the Lord ascended is winding, twisting this way and that [but] whoever wishes to climb up to pray can easily make the ascent.[22]

The concrete specificity of such descriptions links the otherwise abstract theology of Transfiguration to palpable earth. Yet the visionary scope of Transfiguration also embraces the whole created universe. Within the church's normal sacramental life, these cosmic implications of Transfiguration are perhaps best exemplified in the Eucharist. Where, after all, is the co-inherence of Christ's glory and passion or the universal metamorphosis of matter embodied more palpably than in the Eucharistic action centered on bread and wine? Within our own era and Western tradition, the Jesuit priest-scientist Pierre Teilhard de Chardin has explored such connections with rare insight and eloquence. Though church authorities silenced him under suspicion of heterodoxy and pantheism, this French paleontologist and spiritual writer entertained a vivid sense of the Incarnation as a dynamic presence within the extended body of the material world. And Teilhard's "Mass on the World,"

21. Lane, *The Solace*, 124, 258 n3.
22. Ibid., 124, 131.

a prose-poem written in 1923, effectively underscores the Eucharistic aspect of Transfiguration.

As Teilhard explains, "Mass on the World" (though based on earlier writing and later included in a larger collection titled *Hymn of the Universe*) was occasioned by his wanting to celebrate the Eucharist on a certain day while on an expedition in China's Ordos Desert, where he lacked an altar and liturgical elements. He had previously confronted a similar privation, while living in the trenches and serving as a stretcher-bearer in World War I.[23] Hence, he proposes to envision as his altar "the whole earth" and to view as his paten and chalice "the depths of a soul laid widely open to all the forces which . . . converge upon the Spirit" at daybreak. Yet Teilhard does not tell the reader directly that *the* day whose dawning he celebrates in his prayerful prose-poem was apparently August 6, a feast day of which he was particularly fond.[24]

This calendar nexus, once recognized, has much to do with how Teilhard expresses his sense of Christ's interfusion with the whole material cosmos. Just as he understood Creation to be enacted as part of a dynamic, continuous process of evolution, so also he interpreted that process—whereby the world's body becomes the extended body of Christ—as the crowning instance of Transfiguration. The sense of evolution as *transformation* (*la doctrine transformisme*), as an enspirited and organic metamorphosis, is apparent throughout Teilhard's mature writings.

Accordingly, Teilhard conceives the dawning light of August 6 to epitomize Eucharistic transformation as well as global Transfiguration. So regarded, the material world undergoes a regenerative metamorphosis to become diaphanous in the light of Christ. Or, as Teilhard articulates the change:

> No visible tremor marks this inexpressible transformation; and yet mysteriously and in very truth, at the touch of the superstantial Word the immense host which is the universe is made flesh. Through your own incarnation, my God, all matter is henceforth incarnate. . . . Now, Lord, through the consecration of the world

23. As early as 1918, Teilhard had begun to formulate a literary expression that he later reshaped into "The Mass on the World," which was published posthumously as chapter 1 in *Hymn of the Universe*. See King, *Spirit of Fire*, 99–100.

24. Teilhard de Chardin, *Hymn*, 19. In introductory remarks included with the volume, N. M. Wildiers points out the necessary link between "Mass on the World" and the Feast of the Transfiguration, 13.

the luminosity and fragrance which suffuse the universe take on for me the lineaments of a body and a face—in you. . . . If I firmly believe that everything around me is the body and blood of the Word, then for me . . . is brought about the marvelous "diaphany" which causes the luminous warmth of a single life to be objectively discernible in and to shine forth from the depths of every event, every element. . . .[25]

It is sad, I think, that Teilhard's startlingly original synthesis of science and Christian spirituality receives so little notice today. Forbidden by his ecclesiastical superiors to publish his theological works while he was alive, Teilhard received some attention in intellectual circles following his death in 1955 but is now largely forgotten, even by members of his own church. From forbidden to forgotten. Yet Teilhard's mystically integrative vision of spirituality and science is sorely needed by a post-industrial society that yearns to recover contact with the living soul. Many persons who remain affiliated with mainstream churches now accept evolutionary science as a matter of fact, presuming it to be compatible with their religious beliefs but without questioning very deeply just *how* this might be so. They may therefore entertain a vague impression that biblical Christianity must be compromised so as to let faith retreat a step or two, now and then, before each advance of modern reason.

Others, who reject the overwhelming scientific evidence for organic evolution in the name of biblical Christianity, have come to be called "creationists." They feel passionate about rejecting what they take to be a modern erosion of faith and biblical authority. Refusing to accept a compromised Christianity, they insist—with some warrant—on preserving a robust biblical faith that may conflict with present-day secular values. Because they identify the teaching of evolution with wholesale acceptance of scientific materialism, they now seek to challenge such instruction by authorizing the joint consideration of "intelligent design" in school biology courses. Most creationists also seek to preserve a stable, unchanging view of Creation.

Yet the textual literalism of this "creationist" theology is anything but creative. It fixes attention almost exclusively on the opening chapters of Genesis with little account of other scripture, including Saint Paul's witness that Christ engenders a new creation. It substitutes trust in a dead letter of scripture for the Spirit animating the divine Word—a Word

25. Teilhard de Chardin, *Hymn*, 24, 25, 28.

that even Puritan Calvinists in the seventeenth century recognized to be something other than the words printed in their Bibles. It also lacks the authentic gospel sense of urgency, immediacy, and newness—of gratitude for an ever-new and perpetually transfigured creation. Nearly a century after the much-publicized Scopes "monkey" trial of 1925, many creationists still cling to such a fossilized faith—while rejecting actual paleontology—as though it were the last remaining refuge from contemporary godlessness. Sadly, this earnest yet rearguard campaign persists not only in southern Scopes territory, but also in Pennsylvania and throughout other regions of the United States.

By contrast, imaginative interpreters such as Traherne and Teilhard witness to a dynamic, materially textured universe where God continues to dwell and make things new. Testimony to the sacred dynamism of evolutionary change can also be found in the "Spring" chapter of Henry Thoreau's *Walden* (1854). Here Thoreau reflects on the strange patterns of life revealed by particles of sand and clay as they thaw on the slope of a railroad bank near his home in the Concord woods. This thoroughly mundane process, discerned in the transfigurative light of imagination, becomes for Thoreau a revelation of how the Creator was "still at work, sporting on this bank, and with excess of energy strewing his fresh designs about."[26] On the other side of this continent, American naturalist John Muir later rhapsodized on the dynamic marvel of evolving life and landforms he witnessed amid the mountains of California. With the benefit of his studies in geology and evolutionary biology, Muir knew that the apparently inert, unchanging features of this landscape are in constant flux. Despite the seeming solidity of the Sierra Nevada's high peaks, even they belong to the play of continuous creation, since "from form to form, beauty to beauty, ever changing, never resting, all are speeding on with love's enthusiasm, singing with the stars the eternal song of creation."[27]

That Christ Transfigured on the mount becomes an iconic lens of the new creation is most explicitly developed, though, in the writing of latter-day Eastern Orthodox theologians and church leaders, such as Sergei Bulgakov, Bishop Kallistos Ware, Ecumenical Patriarch Bartholomew, and Patriarch Ignatius IV of Antioch.[28] Bulgakov, for ex-

26. Thoreau, *Walden*, 273.

27. Muir, *My First Summer*, 128.

28. A number of relevant statements from Orthodox church leaders have been col-

ample, dean of the Orthodox Theological Academy in Paris until his death in 1944, writes eloquently of the revelation from Mount Tabor:

> What was it that the mountain, and the air, and the sky, and the earth, and the whole world, and Christ's disciples saw? What was the glory that shone round about the apostles? It was a clear manifestation of the Holy Spirit resting upon Christ and in him transfiguring the creation. It was an anticipatory revelation of "a new heaven and a new earth"—of the world transfigured and illumined by beauty. . . . "It is good to be here—very good." This is how the world is created by the divine Providence, though it is not as yet revealed to human contemplation. And yet on Mount Tabor it is revealed already. And this contemplation of the incorruptible, archetypal beauty is the joy of joys, "the perfect joy." This is why the feast of Transfiguration is an anticipation of joy, the feast of beauty.[29]

Among other things, then, Transfiguration comes to describe a new mode of seeing, in which glory suffuses the fleshliness of ordinary life. Glory, represented in biblical tradition as supernal light, streams from and beyond God to enlighten the whole body of creation. Mountain, air, sky, and every living creature become luminescent. In such a light one is moved to declare indeed, as Isaiah did in response to his vision in the Temple, "heaven and earth are full of God's glory."

---

lected in Krueger, *Transfiguring the World.*

29. Bulgakov, "The Exceeding Glory," 191.

PART II

Consequences of a Transfiguration Gospel

4

Death and Transfiguration

To SEE THE WORLD transfigured need not, and indeed should not, mean that we look on it naively oblivious to its pain. Neither does attentiveness to the innate glory of things force us to pretend that we already inhabit an endtime where sin, ugliness, and affliction have been erased. Transfiguration looks toward God's ultimate, all-encompassing redemption without overlooking life's sorrow. In mystical terms, it means seeing beneath apparently solid surfaces into the hidden life of things, or seeing with the inner eye of love. Yet, as we have observed, an awareness of affliction already surrounds the biblical story of Jesus transfigured on the mount. Unlike other ancient tales of a hero's ascent to apotheosis, this peak episode is framed by reminders of the cross. So "Death and Transfiguration," to invoke at this point only the title of Richard Strauss's famous musical tone poem, captures the mixed mood of the gospel records.

The gospel accounts underscore this point that the episode of Jesus' brilliant illumination on high leads directly toward his descent into darkness in Jerusalem. In Luke's version, which speaks of Jesus' "exodus" to be accomplished in Jerusalem, we are reminded explicitly of his impending death. It is fair to suppose that Jesus, unlike his disciples, now anticipates quite consciously a violent conclusion to his earthly ministry. For us, too, death is never so distant from life, or from life's most blissful moments, as we might imagine.

But the essential point here is not simply an antithetical relation between life and death, light and darkness. Jesus' story reveals more than a straightforward, oppositional sequence from creative metamorphosis to deathly dissolution. Christian theology, as elaborated by Saint Paul, insists that death must itself be seen as part of a metamorphic process illuminated by the Resurrection. Moreover, according to Paul in Romans 8, not only human beings but all creation (*ktsis*) as it waits in eager longing for God's saving transformation, participate in this metamorphic process wherein suffering and glory are intermingled.[1] The Transfiguration indeed foreshadows the Resurrection, as exegetes often observe and as the evangelists doubtless understood to be the case. And yet, conversely, it is also germane to appreciate how the Resurrection contains and recalls the Transfiguration. For in the post-resurrection narratives, when the risen Christ appears before his onlookers, he makes a point of displaying his wounds—which are not expunged from the glorified body but transfigured into emblems of triumph. He continues to bear the marks of affliction, even as their meaning changes. The mysterious intermingling of affliction with life's deepest meaning and joys can be recognized, too, throughout much of our own human experience, as well as in countless forms of literary expression.

No modern verse treatment of this theme qualifies as more expressive and theologically probing than T. S. Eliot's *Four Quartets*. Justly renowned for his literary craft, Eliot also displays a searching yet robust religious faith throughout the course of these meditative poems. They are, in the classically Anglican manner of Eliot's own faith commitment, comprehensive in their survey of moods, landscapes, traditions, and patterns of spirituality.

The faith journey of the *Quartets* begins with the speaker's introduction to a beauty—sumptuous, ecstatic, illuminative, innocent, and yet erotic—discovered in the rose garden of "Burnt Norton." Evocative images of wholeness dominate this opening sequence. The hopeful, almost palpable presence of roses merges with impressions of a rising lotus plant, an abrupt influx of sunlight, thrush song, and numinous overtones of an "unheard music." But along the way, particularly in the third section of each quartet, Eliot also traverses sites of "disaffection," "deprivation," doubt, and darkness. One such image of hellish despair appears in the evocation of a London tube ride in section three of "Burnt Norton," while the infirm state of humanity in earth's "hospital" becomes the dominant conceit in section four of "East Coker."[2]

---

1. That the transformation Paul envisions here involves indeed a cosmic redemption, affecting all creatures, is confirmed by theologian Christopher Bryan in his book, *The Resurrection of the Messiah*.

2. Eliot, *Four Quartets*, *The Complete Poems*, 118, 120, 128.

"Little Gidding," the last poem in the sequence, also happens to be the most thoroughly steeped in experiences of strife and affliction. Yet here Eliot articulates his most sublime vision of divine love. This vision at once recollects and metamorphoses previous impressions of the rose, even as it recasts hellfire images of dissolution into Pentecostal flame. Through such poetic enactments of transfiguration, we are able to perceive the spiritual link between apparent opposites, between fire and rose. As the medieval English mystics had written of the soul's becoming at last "oned" with God, so also Eliot concludes *Four Quartets* on a note of universal conjunction:

> And all shall be well and
> All manner of thing shall be well
> When the tongues of flame are in-folded
> Into the crowned knot of fire
> And the fire and the rose are one.[3]

Thus envisioning the transfiguration of both history and nature, Eliot in "Little Gidding" recalls that the locale of his meditations had been steeped not only in Nicholas Ferrar's seventeenth-century community of prayer, but also in the strife of the English Civil War. More surprisingly, he strives to see beneath the immediate atmosphere of violence and terror, set loose around him by incandescent dive bombers during the Second World War, to discern therein God's own Pentecostal fire.

This illuminative vision is not to be mistaken for a comforting illusion. For we see everything, Eliot suggests, in accord with some pattern of expectation and understanding. And to replace our customary perception of mortality, transience, and the defeat of all worldly ambitions with the pattern of a new creation is to witness with fresh light the divinely willed restoration of the world. Or as the poet reflects in some key lines from "Little Gidding":

> . . . History may be servitude,
> History may be freedom. See, now they vanish,
> The faces and places, with the self which, as it could, loved them,
> To become renewed, transfigured, in another pattern.
>
> Sin is Behovely, but
> All shall be well, and
> All manner of thing shall be well. . . .[4]

3. Ibid., 145.
4. Ibid., 142–43.

Eliot's poem testifies, then, to the vision of a Love surrounding affliction, loss, and the disfigurements of history. In the process, it identifies the new pattern of transfigurative perception with Julian of Norwich's familiar assurance that "all shall be well." This tempered faith offers a useful corrective to the once-born optimism expounded by some current schools of creation spirituality. Only in the retrospective light of experience, both personal and collective, is grace given to behold the glory of that transfiguring Christ who is Creation's alpha and omega, beginning *and* end.

Four Quartets, therefore, amounts to a sustained meditation not only on the Incarnation, as is commonly observed, but also on the broader implications of Transfiguration. Although Christ's incarnate presence in the world does not immediately perfect the natural or social order, it does transfigure our sense of the world's identity in the light of awakened imagination. Standing atop the mountaintop in Galilee, Jesus in the gospels occupies the equivalent of what Eliot describes as "the point of intersection of the timeless / With time."[5] In Pauline terms, he stands revealed before his privileged disciples as "the image (*eikon*) of the invisible God" (Col 1:15). By the same token, the artistic icon—whether visual, or poetically verbalized—at once discloses divinity and negates itself behind a cloud of unknowing. Within the fuller span of the *Quartets*, Eliot's transfigurative images demonstrate the essential consonance between the "affirmative way" and "negative way" outlined in mystical tradition. Despite the white radiance surrounding the Transfiguration theophany, its placement in the gospels just before Jesus' descent to Jerusalem and Crucifixion identifies it as a glory in affliction not unlike the "showings" of the divine at the heart of Christ's Passion that were received centuries later by Julian of Norwich. *Four Quartets* encompasses all of this and more.

Understandably, the portrayal of World War II in "Little Gidding" derives chiefly from Eliot's immediate impression of bombs falling on London. Now, after absorbing decades of testimony about the Holocaust and other unspeakable atrocities, we must contemplate the full panoply of horrors raised by this period of history. Among those terrors is one that should permanently mark our remembrance of August 6—branding it, so to speak, as a day of mourning ironically wedded to the feast day of Transfiguration. On that date in 1945, an American B-29, dubbed

5. Eliot, "Dry Salvages," *The Complete Poems*, 136.

the Enola Gay, dropped a single uranium-based bomb over Hiroshima, unleashing unparalleled destruction and confronting humankind with the new, apocalyptic dread of nuclear warfare. Around 70,000 people died at the time of the attack. Several thousand others fell wounded or perished eventually from radiation sickness or aggravated burns. Three days later, when a second, plutonium-based weapon was dropped on Nagasaki, approximately 40,000 people died immediately, and 60,000 more were injured.

From the first, conventional wisdom in the United States has insisted that bombing Hiroshima was not only justifiable, in moral terms, but quite necessary. By this late stage of the conflict, both sides had already fallen to practicing total warfare tactics that included massive bombing of civilian populations. Given Japan's fanatical resistance to surrender despite its military losses, the United States' leadership believed it simply *had* to use the new weapon uniquely at its disposal if a bloody, horribly protracted invasion of Japan were to be avoided. Such an Allied invasion would doubtless have required staggering losses of life—not only for U.S. troops, but for Japanese soldiers and civilians as well. By bringing the war swiftly to its inevitable conclusion, the Hiroshima and Nagasaki bombings were thought to have saved countless lives and, therefore, qualify as humane decisions within the inhumane context of modern warfare. Or so the argument runs.

But there is also, I think, reason to heed those who have voiced skepticism. For one thing, this calculus-of-life argument rests on the authority of a utilitarian ethic as well as the supposition that nations could legitimately choose to wage total war in the first place. It is hard to reconcile either of these supporting points with New Testament ethics— or, for that matter, with the standards traditionally upheld by the *jus in bello* provisions of "just war" teaching. To be sure, combatants in World War II also directed conventional weapons against many noncombatant targets with devastating results. Non-nuclear area bombing throughout Europe and Japan killed far more people than did the two atomic bombs. In that sense, the moral issue raised by Hiroshima is not unique. During the war, several nations besides the United States initiated, or perceived a warrant to replicate, questionable tactics expressive of total warfare. The wartime atrocities charged to Japan, Germany, and the Soviet Union betray a scope of homicidal cruelty beyond previous imagination in the modern world. But such doubtful precedents cannot in themselves serve to justify Hiroshima, much less the second attack on Nagasaki.

Moreover, later evidence casts doubt on the widely held assumption that Japan would never have surrendered without the nuclear attacks or a full-scale invasion of its islands. Some highly respected U.S. military leaders, including Dwight Eisenhower, were never convinced that nuclear attacks on Hiroshima and Nagasaki were necessary. There is cause to believe that defective Allied diplomacy, even more than Japanese recalcitrance, prevented the inevitable surrender from happening sooner. By July of 1945 if not earlier, Japanese civilian leaders, admitting the hopelessness of their cause, may have been willing to settle with the Allies to accept defeat on the sole condition that Japan could retain its Emperor.[6] But the U.S. determination to uphold a doctrine of "unconditional surrender" (in accord with the Potsdam Declaration) and to impress the Soviets with a demonstration of nuclear force eliminated all prospects of negotiating such a resolution in advance—even though, ironically, the victors chose to grant precisely this condition less publicly after the fact. By clinging so tenaciously to its "unconditional surrender" doctrine, Allied leaders thus forfeited the opportunity to seek a promising, mutually acceptable course of resolution for all powers concerned. Even Secretary of War Henry Stimson subsequently acknowledged in his memoirs that "History might find that the United States, by its delay in stating its position [with respect to allowing retention of the Emperor], had prolonged the war."[7]

---

6. Alperovitz presents a detailed examination of these issues, as well as the case against conventional justifications of the nuclear attacks, in *The Decision to Use the Atomic Bomb*. According to Alperovitz, "by July 1945 a combination of assurances for the Emperor and the shock of a Russian declaration of war appeared quite likely to bring about surrender long before an invasion could begin" (643). Besides the pressures associated with U.S. relations to the Soviet Union, a number of other factors seem to have encouraged use of the bomb once it was available. Such factors included the momentum felt by scientists who had worked so hard and long to prepare it, the huge expenditures government leaders had authorized for its production, sentiments of vengeance and racialized contempt for the Japanese, and so on. Admittedly, though, most historians now agree that if other nations involved in the war had managed to produce an atomic bomb, they, too, would have been willing to use it. See also Rotter, *Hiroshima*, esp. 127–76; and Zinn, *Postwar America*, 14–21.

7. Cited in Alperovitz, *The Decision*, 478. As Alperovitz points out (474–5), Acting Secretary of State Joseph Grew expressed comparable retrospective doubts about whether use of the bomb would have been necessary had surrender terms been more reasonably modified at the right time.

But whether or not one regards the Hiroshima bombing as warranted, its annihilating effects—both immediately, and by way of foretelling the new global peril—render it a fitting occasion for mourning. So the world continues to mourn this event of August 6, especially on its anniversary day. It is a time to recall with compassion the unmerited suffering of multitudes, to ponder in broader terms how suffering and death can be precipitated by sin, and to renew humankind's resolution to seek enduring peace. The forms of remembrance still practiced through annual observances at Hiroshima resonate, in fact, with the Death and Transfiguration theme enacted in Christian Eucharistic liturgies on August 6. Hiroshima's rituals of mourning include a dedication of flowers, an interval of silent prayer, a release of doves, and the rekindling of light in the form of floating river lanterns. The occasion's liturgy of the word features a Peace Declaration from the mayor and a kind of *anamnesis* or recollection observance that affirms solidarity with all victims, both living and deceased.

John Hersey's classic study titled *Hiroshima* (1946) includes six personal narratives that invite our further reflection on the interplay—at once ironic and tragically earnest—between Hiroshima and the feast of Transfiguration. One of the survivors profiled in this book is Father Wilhelm Kleinsorge, a German Jesuit who had been residing in a Hiroshima mission complex. Hersey relates that on the fateful morning of August 6, 1945, Father Kleinsorge rose at around 6 a.m. to celebrate daily Mass half an hour later. He and a handful of fellow worshippers knelt on the matted floor of the mission chapel before an altar adorned with silks and embroidery. An alarm siren sounded during his recitation of the concluding prayers; then, at precisely 8:15 a.m., he found his leisure reading interrupted by an unearthly flash of light. Although Hersey does not say so, the scriptural lessons and collects that those gathered with Father Kleinsorge had prayed through at that day's Eucharist must have been those appointed for the Feast of Transfiguration.

In several ways, accounts of the Hiroshima catastrophe suggest a heartrending parody of theophany episodes—including the Transfiguration—represented throughout the Bible. Hersey's horrific narrative abounds in imagery of cloud, wind, light, flood, and fire. As in the Transfiguration episode, the new presence at Hiroshima emerges from a cloud—in this case, an ominous mushroom cloud—and is first perceived as an all-surpassing, noiseless flash of light. One survivor,

Hatsuyo Nakamura, recalls the crucial moment when, as she "stood watching her neighbor, everything flashed whiter than any white she had ever seen." We cannot help hearing in these words a warped echo of how the evangelists describe the transfigured Jesus' garments. Abruptly, then, everything turns dark. Murta-*san*, a Christian housekeeper in Father Kleinsorge's mission, could be heard "crying over and over, '*Shu Jesusu, awaremi tamai!* Our Lord Jesus, have pity on us'"[8]

The specter of misery in Hersey's account becomes all the more affecting by virtue of the silent dignity with which we see most of the stricken enduring their affliction:

> To Father Kleinsorge, an Occidental, the silence in the grove by the river, where hundreds of gruesomely wounded suffered together, was one of the most dreadful and awesome phenomena of his whole experience. The hurt ones were quiet; no one wept, much less screamed in pain; no one complained; none of the many who died did so noisily; not even the children cried; very few people even spoke. And when Father Kleinsorge gave water to some whose faces had been almost blotted out by flash burns, they took their share and then raised themselves a little and bowed to him, in thanks.[9]

Even amid the hellish events at Hiroshima, then, something of divine dignity, beauty, and charity can be glimpsed in these resilient survivors. Hersey recounts many instances in which those who were themselves injured or traumatized labored heroically to assist others. For example, the Reverend Kiyoshi Tanimoto, pastor of the Hiroshima Methodist Church, rushed toward rather than away from the city center following detonation to conduct boat rescue operations and perform other deeds of mercy. Although most hospitals had been destroyed and many physicians killed or disabled, Dr. Terufumi Sasaki worked ceaselessly to minister as best he could—without sleep, without needed medical equipment—to the sea of victims surging into his Red Cross Hospital. Dr. Masakazu Fujii almost miraculously escaped a horrid crucifixion after he had been caught and squeezed between two timbers, his head just above the water, when his hospital was swept into the river. Presently he enlisted help to free two nurses whom he saw in a similar

---

8. Hersey, *Hiroshima*, 10, 16.
9. Hersey, *Hiroshima*, 47–48.

predicament, and soon he located medical supplies with which he could treat other wounded refugees.

Grace and charity can be glimpsed even amid this singular horror. It would not be quite fair to say that they minimized the horror. Yet these qualities do, in some manner, transfigure its meaning within the mystery of Christ's passion and incarnation. Transfiguration also helps to define the significance of Hiroshima's latter-day restoration. The city's renewal of life is manifested, in part, through modern construction and verdant parks. At the same time, Hiroshima's symbolic identity has also been transfigured through the years, metamorphosing from a site of physical catastrophe into the spiritual core of a peace movement extending across the globe. While the city's Peace Memorial Museum remains a permanent fixture of this newer identity, corresponding rituals of commemoration also take place now each August in a number of cities around the world.

Forms of diminishment and loss less spectacular than the human losses in Hiroshima and Nagasaki also mark the experience of every mortal being. Ordinarily, though, humans can at least elect to develop some *response* to the death and diminishment they face. They can *do* something with their diminishment—either to expand the soul by way of cooperating creatively with transfigurative grace or to reduce it by way of evasion, denial, and self-pity.

A worthy illustration from literature of how diminishment can be transfigured appears in the final chapter of *Cry, The Beloved Country*, Alan Paton's best-known novel about South Africa under apartheid. Here the story's protagonist, the Reverend Stephen Kumalo, must endure the immense grief of awaiting the execution at dawn of Absalom, his beloved son. Set morally adrift in Johannesburg, Absalom had fallen under the influence of lawless companions. He ends up shooting the homeowner whose presence startles him in the course of a domestic robbery. When the victim dies, Absalom is convicted of murder and receives a sentence of death by hanging. Stephen cannot even witness this event or comfort his son on the morning of his execution. Absalom is hanged in Pretoria, while Stephen has by then returned from Johannesburg to his home village in Natal. Moreover, Stephen's trip to the great city had confronted him with a whole series of crushing disappointments. He had failed to rescue his sister from the city's corrupting influence, failed to make peace there with his brother. Absalom's death would afflict him not only with the loss of his only son, but also with familial shame as everyone knew that this clergyman's child had murdered a leading benefactor of black Africans.

Still, on the morning of Absalom's death, Stephen manages to transfigure these losses by incorporating them into a universal spirit of prayer. Appropriately, this episode of transfiguration takes place on a mountain, a local peak that Stephen had ascended the night before to keep vigil with and for his son. As dawn approaches, Stephen prays in confession, in thanksgiving, and in compassionate remembrance of all those—including his son—whom he had come to know both at home and through his sad journey to Johannesburg. He prays, too, for "all the people of Africa, the beloved country," whose better future in a multiracial society he can imagine but not experience for himself. Like Moses, he can gaze from the mountain toward such a Promised Land while knowing he would never "see that salvation" during his lifetime.[10] It so happens that neither would Alan Paton live to see South Africa achieve its remarkably nonviolent transition in 1994 to a new order beyond apartheid and white political rule.

Stephen Kumalo does not expunge or forget his sorrow but rises above it, so to speak, as he prays on the mountaintop. Far from evading grief, though, he enters there all the more deeply into the essential mystery of divine compassion—in literal terms, a "suffering with" the other. Thus conjoined with God's consummate compassion in Christ, he knows himself to be united as well with his son at the moment of death as well as with the whole communion of saints. As dawn breaks, Stephen finds his losses transfigured in the light of Resurrection. It is fitting that such transfiguration should occur in the context of his celebrating a version of Eucharist:

> He looked out of his clouded eyes at the faint steady lightening in the east. But he calmed himself, and took out the heavy maize cakes and the tea, and put them upon a stone. And he gave thanks, and broke the cakes and ate them, and drank of the tea. Then he gave himself over to deep and earnest prayer, and after each petition he raised his eyes and looked to the east. And the east lightened and lightened, till he know that the time was not far off. And when he expected it, he rose to his feet and took off his hat and laid it down on the earth, and clasped his hands before him. And while he stood there the sun rose in the east.[11]

10. Paton, *Cry, The Beloved Country*, 310.
11. Paton, *Cry, the Beloved Country*, 312.

That loss can be transfigured by the way one chooses to respond to life's diminishment likewise figures in texts emerging from non-Christian religious traditions. This theme is especially prominent in Buddhist teaching. *The Snow Leopard*, Peter Matthiessen's account of his arduous journey through Himalayan heights of Nepal, could serve as one example. During much of the trip, Matthiessen had hoped to meet the revered Lama of Shey at a holy place known as the Crystal Monastery. Reaching the monastery, Matthiessen is disappointed to find that its lama and monks had vacated the site. When he finally does encounter the holy man, he finds the lama had not only become physically disabled, but had been obliged to live in isolation for some eight years. Yet he appears contented. Asked how he feels about his forced seclusion, the lama gives a startling reply:

> And this holy man of great directness and simplicity, big white teeth shining, laughs out loud in an infectious way at Jang-bu's question. Indicating his twisted legs without a trace of self-pity or bitterness, as if they belonged to all of us, he casts his arms wide to the sky and the snow mountains, the high sun and dancing sheep, and cries, "Of course I am happy here! It's wonderful! *Especially* when I have no choice!"[12]

This remark runs squarely against the assumption, enforced by the secular materialism of Western culture, that our happiness and freedom depend on gaining access to an unlimited range of appealing life options. No wonder Matthiessen writes that upon hearing this remark, laden with "wholehearted acceptance of *what is*," he felt as though the holy man "had struck me in the chest."[13] The lama radiates an interior peace that derives from his transfiguration of drastic limitation. How has he achieved this? Not, I think, by a grimly stoic resolve so much as by going with the flow. His laughter springs from a self-transcending spirit of good humor, which helps him remain creatively attentive to the hidden graces of his situation.

Inevitably, then, inquiry into the relation between death and transfiguration leads toward questions of practical spirituality. To explore this dimension of metamorphosis, one naturally looks to profit from the wisdom of selected guides—including, once again, Pierre Teilhard de Chardin—within the church's longstanding tradition of contemplative prayer.

12. Matthiessen, *The Snow Leopard*, 246.

13. Ibid.

5

Toward a Spirituality of Transfiguration

A TRANSFIGURATION GOSPEL CASTS new light not only on our theologies of creation and of human nature, but on spiritual praxis as well. This devotional consequence of metamorphosis is evident in writings by Traherne, Teilhard de Chardin, and other figures considered thus far. It is also highlighted by the author of Luke's gospel, when he shows how Jesus' prayer issues in transfiguration. Seeking an interval of escape from the crowds, Jesus ascends the mountain in Galilee to commune with the Father. In Matthew's account, the three disciples then fall to the ground in worshipful awe, as they see Jesus mysteriously transformed. This posture is frequently displayed in Orthodox icons of the scene. So Jesus' prayer ends up inspiring further prayer. That has been happening ever since. The church's pattern of collective prayer, particularly as enacted in the Eucharist, amounts to a participation in the transforming life and death of the Risen Lord. A Transfiguration gospel therefore influences our understanding both of common liturgy and of personal prayer.

At base, the theology of prayer suggested by the Transfiguration event is remarkably simple. To be sure, there must have been some personal variations in how the three disciples responded spiritually to this theophany. So far as we know, James and John remained silent throughout the entire episode. The crucial invitation to all three disciples was simply to *behold* the sacred mystery set before them. They had only to absorb it inwardly as best they could. For the moment, despite Peter's nervousness, they were not called to say or do anything else. To "behold" the vision in its fullness, to stand silently before the face of God, is everything. To "behold" so as to conjoin one's whole heart and will with that vision poses more than enough challenge to ordinary human faculties. So I think it fitting, then, that Matthew inserts the dramatic pause of "behold" (*idou*, in Matt 17:3) before announcing the appearance of Moses and Elijah, though the word is rarely included in English translations.[1]

It is fitting, too, that the evangelists end their account of this theophany on a note of dramatic concentration, with the disciples focused on Jesus alone. This detail reinforces the sense of progressing inwardly toward a radical simplification of one's attention. It confirms the principle of aspiring toward a consonance of will among all six figures in the tableau. Such consonance between human and divine orders of being corresponds, in turn, to the ideal of Christian prayer. Evelyn Underhill, commenting on the petition that "thy will be done" in the Lord's Prayer, observes how this self-abandoning entreaty captures the essence of all prayer, because "only 'in Christ' are the Absolute Will and the will of the creature plaited together, to make a single cord of love."[2]

"Thy will be done"—a pledge so casually declared in recitation, so agonizingly elusive in practice. Prayer techniques commended by Saint Gregory Palamas and other Hesychastic teachers offered one means of participating in that process of self-transformation. No wonder, then, that the spirituality of Hesychasm came to be identified with the uncreated but recreative light of the Transfiguration.

The principle of radical simplification represented in the disciples' seeing all in "Jesus himself alone" (Matt 17:8) is likewise apparent in Hesychasm's embrace of the Jesus Prayer. The formula itself, often supported by deliberate breathing, is elemental. What could be simpler than repeating, over and over again, "Lord Jesus Christ, Son of God, have mercy on me"? Yet this repetition, by its very nature, underscores the mystical meaning of transformation: the human subject changes, becoming all the more "oned" with God, while these spoken words—like the divine Word—remain the same.

In our own day, too, spiritual directors often recognize that repeated invocation can, in the words of Russian Orthodox Metropolitan Anthony Bloom, "be used systematically to achieve an inner transformation." Such techniques, which could also involve controlled breathing and other bodily components, were particularly favored by Gregory Palamas and other champions of the fourteenth-century Hesychastic tradition. For these monastics, the Transfiguration affirmed that it was

1. Lee, *Transfiguration*, 47.
2. Underhill, *Practical Mysticism*, 183.

possible indeed for humans, under grace but in this life, to encounter the uncreated light of God.[3] "More than any other prayer," avers Bishop Bloom, "the Jesus Prayer aims at bringing us to stand in God's presence with no other thought but the miracle of our standing there and God with us, because in the use of the Jesus Prayer there is nothing and no one except God and us." Again we are reminded how, at the close of their mountaintop vision, the three disciples are struck to be seeing at that point no one—except Jesus and themselves. Scripture's iconic tableau of the Transfiguration affords something comparable to what Bloom attributes to the Jesus Prayer: "a focus that allows us to keep our attention still in the presence of God."[4]

Another important spiritual charism, best signified by the over-shadowing cloud,[5] has been described in contemplative tradition as "detachment." Properly understood, such detachment implies neither indifference toward the common lot of humanity nor the repression of feeling. It relates instead to the soul's progress under grace toward authentic liberty. To attain this condition, one must free oneself from egotism, anxiety, and every form of addiction. As the disciples climbed with Jesus to the mountain summit, they must have carried with them the usual human burdens of worry, disappointment, and doubt. But despite their momentary fear under the cloud, the weight of their earthly anxieties falls away once the vision takes hold. The vision's beauty takes them out of themselves and into the Presence who is "all in all," abruptly detaches them from egotism. As the divinely revealing yet veiling atmosphere of the cloud suggests, they witness something they do not know: they only know it to surpass anything they have yet known or imagined. Its transcendent character is underscored first by Mark's description of garments whiter than white. Then, according to Matthew and Luke, all human words and images—epitomized by Peter's speech—are effectively blotted out as the disciples are taken under the cloud. Thus, the cloud reinforces the apophatic, or "negative way," principle of spirituality that insists on the surpassing, ultimately indescribable character of such an

---

3. Stevenson, *Rooted in Detachment*, 107–11. Hughes, in *Beloved Dust*, points out that for Palamas and other Hesychastic monks, transfigurative contemplation involved the whole person, so as to include bodily elements, 262.

4. Bloom, *Living Prayer*, 88.

5. For a thoughtful commentary on possible significances of the cloud, see Stevenson's *Rooted in Detachment*, 97–112.

experience. Even had the disciples been authorized to tell others what they had seen, they would never have found the right words to do so. For that matter, even the gospel accounts of the episode relate this all-surpassing experience to us only indirectly, not as first-hand testimony but as a recollection of impressions conveyed from those who were there.

Yet those who were there keep this momentous event to themselves for some time. In accord with other gospel exhortations of messianic secrecy, Jesus orders them to refrain from relating the encounter to others "until after the Son of Man had risen from the dead" (Mark 9: 9). So they must not only come down from the mountain, descending all too abruptly from their peak experience to face a troubled crowd, but must also ponder the episode's meaning in relative isolation. Unable to test the reality of their perceptions with those outside their select circle, they faced an inward struggle to assimilate all that had happened. They remain in some sense "apart, by themselves," as they had been at the time of their ascent.

But again, and yet again and again in figurative terms, they had to come down from the mountain. As their glimpse of glory fades, they face once more life's failures and diminishments—for themselves, as well as in relation to others. Their very first challenge to serve as agents of the metamorphosis they have witnessed, on behalf of that spirit-troubled and convulsive child, ends in failure.

In *The Divine Milieu*, Teilhard de Chardin expounds at length on the spiritual challenge of diminishment. In the work as a whole, he charts a spiritual process he perceives as leading toward "*a total transformation of ourselves and of everything surrounding us.*"[6] This process of what he calls "divinisation" encompasses both the "activities" and "passivities" of human experience—what we do, as well as what we undergo or endure. Teilhard claims that to dwell solely on what we do, by direct volition, takes us only "halfway along the road which leads to the mountain of the Transfiguration."[7] In fact, life's toughest challenges may involve confronting and accepting our passivities. That is particularly so when what happens to us registers not as a growth experience but as diminishment. The many deaths and failures that constitute a human life can threaten to kill one's spirit. In broader social perspective, the misery of those afflicted by disease, calamity, war, or poverty is striking enough. While set-

6. Teilhard de Chardin, *The Divine Milieu*, 103.

7. Ibid., 71.

ting forth his spirituality of transformation, Desmond Tutu elaborates on this theme, as we shall see in chapter 8, in *God Has a Dream: A Vision of Hope for Our Time*. Yet as Teilhard observes, all persons must confront diminishments of their humanity:

> All of us one day or another will come to realize, if we have not already done so, that one or other of these sources of disintegration has lodged itself in the very heart of our lives. Sometimes it is the cells of the body that rebel or become diseased; at other times the very elements of our personality seem to be in conflict or to detach themselves from any sort of order. And then we impotently stand by and watch collapse, rebellion, and inner tyranny, and no friendly influence can come to our help. And if by chance we escape, to a greater or lesser extent, the critical forms of these assaults from without which appear deep within us and irresistibly destroy the strength, the light and the love by which we live, there still remains that slow, essential deterioration which we cannot escape: old age little by little robbing us of ourselves and pushing us on toward the end. Time, which postpones possession, time which tears us away from enjoyment, time which condemns us all to death—what a formidable passivity is the passage of time. . . .
>
> In death, as in an ocean, all our slow or swift diminishments flow out and merge. Death is the sum and consummation of all our diminishments.[8]

Teilhard was personally acquainted with many such diminishments. He was acutely aware that one's sense of self could be eroded by inward privations and disappointment, no less than by the outward assaults of illness and disease. And his own life afforded him ample exposure to such psychic forms of grief. Forbidden by authorities of the Roman curia and of his own Jesuit order from publishing his theological writings, he endured decades of misunderstanding and official rejection. He found this failure to gain fair hearing for his ideas immensely frustrating—so frustrating, in fact, that one might well have expected him to defy his censors and the shortsightedness of his superiors by abandoning the priesthood. Honoring his vow of obedience could scarcely have been easy. What's more, he found himself by 1932 deeply in love with an American artist named Lucille Swan, an attachment whose sexual fulfillment would have violated his vow of priestly celibacy.[9]

8. Teilhard de Chardin, *The Divine Milieu*, 81–82.

9. King, *Spirit of Fire*, 144–54. Throughout her book *For the Time Being*, Dillard also offers poignant reflections on the distinctive adversities Teilhard endured, esp. 102–5,

But instead of claiming his freedom and right to free expression elsewhere, in another sphere, Teilhard resolved to remain faithful. Instead of escaping his strictures by finding a new vocation and condition, he aimed to cooperate with divine grace by welcoming a transformation *from within* of his old life. Accepting with grace the misfortunes of disdain, exile, and loneliness throughout much of his career, he was virtually forgotten by the time he died in New York, where his body lies today in an obscure gravesite situated on the grounds of a culinary school.

Clearly, then, the theological hope that Teilhard manifests in his writings cannot be attributed either to naive optimism or to worldly good fortune. Such hope derives rather from Teilhard's resurrectional faith, a faith that affirmed the ultimate reality of personal and cosmic transformation. Teilhard aimed to re-envision the world as a divine milieu, "a zone of continuous spiritual transformation"[10] within which God transfigures into glory even our failures and diminishments. If the Transfiguration is a feast of beauty, it displays for Teilhard a creator who qualifies as the consummate artist:

> Like an artist who is able to make use of a fault or an impurity in the stone he is sculpting or the bronze he is casting so as to produce more exquisite lines or a more beautiful tone, God, without sparing us the partial deaths, nor the final death, which form an essential part of our lives, transfigures them by integrating them in a better plan—*provided we lovingly trust in him.* . . . Not everything is immediately good to those who seek God; but everything is capable of becoming good: *omnia convertuntur in bonum.*[11]

Often, though, the processes of transformation operate slowly, secretly, through fits and starts. Cosmic transformation, which Teilhard imagined proceeding at last toward an omega point in which God becomes all in all, would be discernible only on the grander scale of geological or astronomical time. It was typically by faith, rather than by what Teilhard could observe directly, that he was inspired to believe that "at the heart of the divine milieu, as the church reveals it, things are transfigured, but from within"[12]—and in a manner that preserved their distinctive attributes and individuality. In the meantime, life in the

---

181–85, and 192–95.

10. Teilhard de Chardin, *The Divine Milieu*, 124–25.

11. Ibid., 86.

12. Ibid., 118.

spirit requires not only faith, but considerable patience, discipline, and perseverance.

Consider, for example, the sort of metamorphosis or transfiguration we might expect from prayers of petition. Does petitionary or intercessory prayer actually *change* anything? And if so, does it exercise a transformative influence only sometimes, or always—but unpredictably and indiscernibly? It is fair to wonder. In Mark Twain's best-known novel, Huck Finn becomes understandably skeptical when his prayers of entreaty for fishhooks yield not even a nibble of success. Some consider it vain to suppose that prayer could have any outward effect, in the sense of changing God's mind or will. Its effects are said to be wholly interior, restricted to changes of heart in the one who prays. Others suggest that while prayer draws souls toward inward conformity with God's will, it might also have some co-creative bearing on how things unfold—just as other, more material forms of human initiative plainly affect the course of events.

In either case, the very act of prayer presupposes belief in the possibility of metamorphosis. *Something* changes or is changed on account of prayer. Unless we can affirm this much, prayer amounts to nothing more than superstition or wishful thinking. At the least, we can hope to see prayer transform our perception of things, or to change our felt relation to circumstances we cannot change. Ordinarily, such transfigurations in the spiritual domain occur gradually. The vision on Mount Tabor discloses in a flash that endpoint of divinisation toward which humanity—and all creation—aspires. Teilhard believed that attaining this endpoint implies a collective evolution of human spirituality and consciousness in a transbiological realm he called the "noosphere." A version of what Teilhard envisioned as this larger evolutionary path is mirrored in the spiritual journeying of individuals.

For an individual, too, reaching the summit of communion with glory takes more than an afternoon's climb. In real time, the process of ascending toward this peak requires patience, repeated effort, and a sustained commitment. If in Luke's account Jesus retreats to the mountain for the express purpose of praying, it is also evident that even he persists in communicating with the Father, both before and after this episode. Far from ending the need for prayer, the Transfiguration dramatizes its ultimate potential—and its role as a perpetual, ongoing practice even for the Christ. Accordingly, Luke tells us that Jesus exhorts his disciples through a parable concerning "their need to pray always and not to lose heart" (Luke 18:1).

The Transfiguration epitomizes mystical prayer insofar as it enacts the hope of beholding—in ourselves, to begin with—a radical opening toward transformation. Saint Paul describes this transformation as occurring not through imposition of our own interceding will but through the Spirit's interceding for us and within us "with sighs too deep for words" (Rom 8:26). Beholding God, we can by degrees change to image that glory so far as we allow "the light of the knowledge of the glory of God in the face of Jesus Christ" to shine in our hearts (2 Cor 4:6). True prayer thus differs from magic, which seeks by human craft to manipulate and refashion reality in accord with our own image. And as Robert Hughes points out, transfiguration aptly describes a second tidal movement of the Spirit within us, equivalent to what has classically been described as the illuminative phase of interior development.[13]

We notice readily enough how ill fortune can turn good persons into far less appealing and generous colleagues. But with the benefit of all we know today about genetics and the long-term effects of childhood nurture, we are apt to doubt that mature adults really are, or can be, permanently transformed into something better—through prayer or any other means. Present-day media impressions from popular culture often betray skepticism about the validity of moral and spiritual transformations that seem out of character. Must not these changes prove as illusory and transitory as the results of most weight-loss programs? A spirituality of transfiguration challenges this skepticism head-on. So does much in our inherited literary tradition. Consider, for example, Shakespeare's hopeful drama of sea changes in *The Tempest*—a tale of lost souls who are eventually found and of bad guys who end up behaving much better than where they'd started.

"See, I am making all things new" (Rev 21:5). With these words, according to John of Patmos, the Lord of life describes the ultimate course of creation. "Making all things new"—this motto aptly summarizes what the Transfiguration illustrates in dramatic terms. Trusting that authentically new things can emerge from what is old may not come easily, but such faith in creative metamorphosis is itself regenerative. Perhaps, as Arnold Benz points out, reflection on the material processes observed by astronomers gives credence to the idea that new things continue, even now, to be created from old things.

---

13. Hughes, *Beloved Dust*, esp. 257–310.

Again it is instructive to see how *Four Quartets*, the last major work T. S. Eliot published, embodied this poet's conviction that growth and genuine change are possible even in older phases of one's life.[14] In "East Coker," the second section of *Four Quartets*, he insists, as though preaching to himself, that "Old men ought to be explorers."[15] And in "Little Gidding," the climactic poem of the sequence, he portrays his explorer as responding to a call—as neither instigating the journey nor determining its precise course. Echoing the anonymous mystical author of the fourteenth-century *Cloud of Unknowing*, Eliot finds this new adventure inspired instead by "the drawing of this Love and the voice of this Calling." The way he imagines leads the soul at once forward, toward its destiny, and back to primal origins:

> We shall not cease from exploration
> And the end of all our exploring
> Will be to arrive where we started
> And know the place for the first time.
> Through the unknown, unremembered gate
> When the last of earth left to discover
> Is that which was the beginning. . . .[16]

Over the decades since they were written, these lines have resonated profoundly with many pilgrims of the spirit. Not long ago, they assumed special meaning for me when I moved with my family—for family rather than professional reasons—from Connecticut to Tennessee. I found the move unsettling in more than one respect. As a lifelong Yankee with firm roots in northeastern Connecticut, I feared the loss of familiar scenes and routines. I would be leaving a satisfying, tenured faculty position in Connecticut to embrace an uncertain future. No definite job awaited me in Tennessee. I wondered if I would ever discover a home and new vocation there, on what locals call "the Mountain" of Sewanee. What's more, I grieved at the thought of losing touch with cherished friends, university colleagues, and parishioners at the nearby Episcopal Church where my wife had long served as parish priest.

One such parishioner-friend had presented herself for confirmation shortly before unforeseen events led us to think about leaving

---

14. Fuller discussion of Eliot's complex poetic responses to aging can be found in Brooker, "Youth and Age," 465–83.

15. Eliot, *Four Quartets*, 129.

16. Eliot, *Four Quartets*, 145.

Connecticut. I felt honored to be Judith's confirmation sponsor. In this role, I spoke briefly at a parish celebration about Judith and the circumstances that eventually brought her to adult confirmation. I reflected on the graced irony that she had lately returned to northeastern Connecticut, her birthplace and childhood home, just as she had lately "come home" to a deeper understanding of faith through the convoluted course of her life journey. Recalling Judith's involvement in literary culture, I thought it fitting then to cite Eliot's words about arriving where we started and knowing it for the first time.

That was in the spring of 2004. My wife had already toured Sewanee, Tennessee, with a realtor to arrange for purchase of a property I had never seen. As summer approached, we prepared to move South and to conclude our affairs in Connecticut. In the meantime, Judith had been staying in Charlottesville, Virginia, venturing once briefly from there to visit the Tennessee town where we would be living. In a letter to us, she described visiting this village and its picturesque sandstone buildings on the University of the South campus. Near the center of town she had wandered into an unlocked cottage, apparently for sale and in dreadful repair. And she reported finding there, painted on an upstairs wall, the same Eliot lines I had invoked for our parish celebration.

"How about that!" I remarked to my wife, as I read Judith's letter. "What an extraordinary coincidence." "Not only that," she replied, smiling, "but you should know that I recognize the house she visited to be *ours*, the one we've just bought and that you've never seen."

When workers we hired to improve the house in advance of our arrival whitewashed the upstairs walls, they decided—without instruction from us—to paint around the poetic inscription. So these black-etched words remain fixed in what is now our daughter's bedroom, as I never fail to notice when I ascend the stairs:

> We shall not cease from exploration
> And the end of all our exploring
> Will be to arrive where we started
> And know the place for the first time.[17]

What does this have to do with Transfiguration? In one sense, the story of our lives is one of cumulative loss. Beyond childhood, we can expect to lose our youth—and eventually our jobs, health, friendships,

---

17. Eliot, "Little Gidding," *Four Quartets*, 145.

and life itself. Yet faith envisions this inevitable close as opening toward some further purpose, or "end," of enigmatic depth. In the light of transfiguration, nothing is ever wholly lost but is transformed into something else. So each person's life journey may, despite its diminishments, trace a circular or cyclic rather than strictly linear path. And we may find in the *telos*, or spiritual end, of this exploration a startling transfiguration of its initiation.

Thus, Eliot's experience of coming home to the village of Little Gidding is one I could appreciate. When the poet visited there in spring of 1936, he had never resided in this place, the site of a semi-monastic Anglican religious community founded by Nicholas Ferrar in the seventeenth century. Yet he felt himself drawn into what was evidently sacred space, a place "where prayer has been valid."[18] As such, Little Gidding ended up speaking deeply to him, not only of historical precedents but of his own origins, faith inquiry, and destiny. So for Eliot, the visit offered considerably more than a tourist attraction.

Only later, after I had lived a year or two in Sewanee, did I start to understand how "knowing a place for the first time" may mean discovering strangeness in that which I took to be familiar—and, paradoxically, finding a home place in that which once seemed alien. Impressions of this sort are, I suppose, what Freud had in mind when describing his theory of the uncanny. "It is good for us to be here" (Mark 9:5)—that conclusion Peter got quite right during his visit to one mountain, and so I came to feel about relocating my home on another. And as I learned more about William Porcher DuBose, a leading theologian of the Episcopal Church who figured prominently in Sewanee's nineteenth-century history, I was intrigued to discover that for him, too, local topography had once inspired thoughts of biblical proportion. In chapter 9, I discuss a sermon DuBose preached on the Transfiguration wherein he associates the scriptural peak quite explicitly with the "holy mountain" of Sewanee.

What else might we draw for ourselves from Peter's remark in the gospel accounts that "it is good for us to be here," on the holy mountain? In fact this simple statement, if we appreciate its depth and can pronounce it in our own lives, voices an ideal outcome of transfigurative spirituality. Though God once declared globally, according to Genesis, that this earth is "good," we must often travel far in spirit and time before achieving a personal, locally grounded conviction that "It is good for us

18. Eliot, *Four Quartets*, 139.

to be here" on whatever plot of earth we call "home." Whenever we find ourselves longing to live somewhere else, or at some other time, it is a strain to believe this. "It is good for us to be here" is thus a fitting theme for meditation, as it sets before us a hope compounded at once of acceptance and of transformation.

6

Liturgies, Festivals, and the Prospect of a Transfigurative "Earth Day"

CORPORATE AND SACRAMENTAL FORMS of worship offer yet another way of entering a spirituality of transfiguration. The Eucharist, as noted in previous chapters, is a prime illustration of what transformation might mean. Whether or not one endorses transubstantiation or another discrete theory of how transformation occurs, this sacrament clearly dramatizes a metamorphosis. For believers, the bread and wine they consume become something other than ordinary food. Jesus at the Last Supper declared himself henceforth accessible to his friends through a novel mode of material presence. And a broad spectrum of Christian churches today understand the Eucharist to enact not only some "real" presence of the resurrected Lord, but also a process of transformation. Even those who favor a highly Protestant or "receptionist" interpretation of the Eucharistic action hope that partakers of the sacrament—if not the material elements themselves—undergo an inward change. One could argue, in fact, that performing any sacramental act displays some hope for transformation. Otherwise, the ritual has no purpose.

But what has been the character and purpose of liturgies dedicated specifically to the Transfiguration? And what prospects for fuller commemoration might one wish to see developed in the future? Could a Day of Transfiguration eventually be recognized as the Christian counterpart of Earth Day? It seems to me that such an idea, which has already been suggested in passing,[1] bears a potential worth examining in relation to these other questions.

---

1. By Dowell, for example, who in turn credits Sean McDonagh for this suggestion in Dowell's *Enjoying the World*, 123.

CURRENT STATUS OF THE FEAST DAY LITURGIES

In Byzantine Christianity, the Transfiguration has long enjoyed comparatively high recognition as one of the Church's twelve great feasts. Even in the East, however, it rarely draws as much attention as it deserves, given its sweeping theological significance.[2] In the Latin Church, it had been celebrated liturgically in diverse ways and places for at least five centuries before 1456, when Rome called for general observance of the feast on August 6. It had also been observed in the West, at least by way of lectionary readings, on the Second Sunday in Lent.

Today the Transfiguration continues to be observed on August 6, at least on the books, by Roman Catholic, Anglican, Eastern Orthodox, and many Lutheran churches. In the wake of liturgical renewal, it has also been recognized by several denominations in the form of Eucharistic lectionary readings designated for the Last Sunday after the Epiphany. It appears thus in the *Revised Common Lectionary* issued in 1992 and is often identified as "Transfiguration Sunday." But for most practicing Christians in the West, to say nothing of the unchurched, this feast day remains an obscure or unknown commemoration.

To review briefly the history of its observance in Anglican tradition is instructive by way of illustration. Within the Anglican Communion, the U.S. Episcopal Church led the way in restoring August 6 to red-letter calendar status back in 1886. Before this effort, led by William Reed Huntington, the Transfiguration found even less place in the church's liturgical year. It was not even restored as a black-letter day until 1561.[3] True, Michael Ramsey's study shows that an Anglican tradition of homiletic exegesis had developed around the relevant texts, a tradition numbering such prominent figures as Joseph Hall in the seventeenth century and F. D. Maurice in the nineteenth.[4] As we have seen, a rich legacy of literary reflection by individual Anglican and other Western writers surrounds the imaginative theme of Transfiguration. Moreover, a fair number of parishes, as well as some religious orders and other bodies within the Anglican Communion, identify themselves by title with the Transfiguration. The 1979 U.S. *Book of Common Prayer* now lists its commemorative day on August 6 among the ten most important

---

2. Such is likewise the conclusion voiced by Andreopoulos in *Metamorphosis*, 15.

3. Hatchett, *Commentary*, 70.

4. Ramsey, *The Glory of God.*

feasts on its calendar, though not among its seven "principal feasts," or among the first five, as in the Eastern Church. Yet genuine celebration of the feast as festival, complete with paraliturgical practices and customs, has never been part of this tradition in the West. It is still exceedingly rare for parishes, schools, summer programs, and other church-related bodies to make much—or, indeed, to make anything at all—of August 6 when it comes to highlighting liturgical observances that could be conjoined with community gatherings.

This omission cannot be blamed on a lack of materials in the 1979 *Book of Common Prayer*. The day's special Collect, written by William Reed Huntington,[5] strikes a penetrating note with its entreaty that we might "by faith behold the King in his beauty." Moreover, the Eucharistic lections and daily office readings for August 6 offer a wealth of verbal iconography for reflection and preaching. Beyond the resources already available in the 1928 Prayer Book, the 1979 Book includes as well a set of Evening Prayer lections for the Eve of the Transfiguration.

The 1982 Hymnal supports this development insofar as it adds two musical settings each for two relevant hymns ("O Light of Light," 133 and 134; and "Christ upon the Mountain Peak," 129 and 130) beyond the single pertinent hymn on a fifteenth-century text ("O Wondrous Type! O Vision Fair," 136 and 137) that was included in the previous 1940 collection. It seems to me unfortunate, however, that the 1982 collection no longer accords the Transfiguration feast day a separate physical space, as had been the case in 1940 and as continues to be provided for feasts such as the Ascension, the Annunciation, and even St. Joseph's day. In fact, hymns that might be sung for the Transfiguration feast day are so scattered throughout the current hymnal, mostly within the Epiphany section, that nobody except savvy church musicians or clerics armed with a separate index volume will notice them at all. Any view of this feast day as a discrete liturgical occasion has thus been obscured to the vanishing point. This drawback could be remedied, with little effort, in the hymnal's next edition.

One reason, of course, why little or nothing happens liturgically on August 6 is that this fixed date usually falls on a weekday, rather than in the Sunday slot that our mainstream culture regards as the only acceptable day of worship aside from Christmas. Other important days of commemoration, including those dedicated to the Ascension, All

---

5. Hatchett, *Commentary*, 70, 204.

Saints, and the Annunciation, suffer this same neglect. What's more, most church-related schools above the equator that might be inclined to observe the Transfiguration are not in session during the summer. Given these circumstances, one may feel little cause to worry about which hymn choices are available for August 6. If very few churches mark this date with some form of liturgy, even fewer consider the occasion worth employing an organist to provide service music or to support hymnody. Accordingly, the idea of transferring its observance to the last Sunday of Epiphany seems appealing. And it does make some theological sense. Since the Transfiguration can be interpreted as the climactic episode of epiphany, the day's Sunday lections offer souls a moment of glory to recall just before their sobering descent into Lent.

Yet this newly instituted Sunday observance has failed, on balance, to heighten general awareness of the feast's significance. In theory, the variably dated Sunday observance complements, rather than replaces, the observance on August 6. In practice, though, neither date registers in the minds of most communicants. Why not? Perhaps it's because the ambiguity of this observance, divided as it is between two different dates, blurs the focus of attention. Perhaps it's because in mainstream American culture, as distinguished from certain ethnic subcultures, no exclusively church-designated feast day aside from Pentecost draws much attention or figures seriously in parish life. That is true even for commemorations assigned to Sunday.

In fact, the Sunday, end-of-Epiphany liturgy simply cannot, as now defined, become a genuine festival of the Transfiguration because it is—unlike August 6—no feast day at all. What it amounts to instead is just another Epiphany Sunday to which scriptural lections related to the Transfiguration have been assigned. That circumstance is quite different, liturgically, from a feast such as Pentecost or Trinity Sunday. The calendar designation in *The Book of Common Prayer*, for example, leaves no doubt about that. Grass-roots practices confirm this impression. Most parishes do not, either verbally (in their bulletins or newsletters) or visually (through use of white vestments, for example) identify the Sunday in question as "Transfiguration Day."

But if churches in the West did recognize the need to recover and to heighten celebration of such a day, enlarging on its potential as a festival of creation, how might they pursue this end? All things considered, which single date of observance makes the most sense, both practically and liturgically? This question may need to be considered first. Three possibilities come most readily to mind.

1. Preserve but enlarge and redefine the commemoration on Epiphany's closing Sunday so that it becomes a recognizable feast day, comparable, for example, to the Baptism of Our Lord.

2. Preserve August 6 as the central day of commemoration but heighten its celebration on this day, both liturgically and through community festivities.

3. Preserve August 6 as the "official" date of observance but encourage transfer of liturgical and other commemorations to the first Sunday thereafter.

Outside monastic and other select communities, the second of these prospects probably cannot be achieved, for reasons already indicated. The first option may be most plausible, though it requires forfeiting seasonal traditions that have developed around the August 6 observance, including earth-linked associations with the harvest rituals of late summer. At least in northern temperate climates, a late winter Transfiguration Day assumes a very different character, one detached from the agricultural customs now attached, albeit tenuously, to August 6. As a moveable feast, a Transfiguration Day situated on last Epiphany is also harder to etch into collective memory than a fixed date. What is more, neither the Roman Catholic Church nor most Eastern Orthodox churches now assign lections for the Transfiguration to last Epiphany, a time that Roman Catholics designate instead as part of a cycle within "ordinary time." These two major bodies must be involved in any joint liturgical initiative that aspires to influence society.

The third option also shows some promise. Roman Catholic practice already permits the transfer to Sunday of some major feasts. For the Episcopal Church, such an observance would require only minor rubrical change in *The Book of Common Prayer*, as August 6 already qualifies therein as one of three feasts that "take precedence of a Sunday."[6]

---

6. That is, a feast whose lections displace those otherwise ordered for the day when August 6 falls on Sunday.

PROSPECTS FOR A CHRISTIAN "EARTH DAY"

In light of the current environmental crisis, it is encouraging to learn that the Earth Day commemoration of April 22 has been called the most popular secular festival day in the world, with perhaps half a billion people each year observing it in some manner.[7] The occasion, inspired by Senator Gaylord Nelson of Wisconsin, was first celebrated by Americans in 1970. Since then, it has won international favor. It began as something of a revivalistic, grass-roots teach-in and continues to emphasize ties between environmental education and activist ideals of social reform. Today it is often marked by festivities, symbolic gestures, and rituals, including tree plantings, the performance of earth songs, fairs and processions, and displays of banners and distinctive clothing. The communal vitality evidenced by these rituals is encouraging. It is less encouraging to notice how rarely faith communities have been involved in organizing such activities. In other contexts, one might have expected church bodies to take a lead in the ritualizing of belief. Rituals and processions are, after all, something that faith communities know how to do. But in the case of Earth Day, it is secular organizers who have instead taken the lead in dramatizing the need for a sacred housekeeping of earth. Religious leaders have, on occasion, been disposed to talk about environmental matters but without, for the most part, marking their significance on some liturgical occasion.

If something like a Christian earth day were to be designated liturgically or to be attached to an existing feast day, what occasion would best suit this purpose? An entirely novel observance, with no roots in tradition or scripture, would be ill-advised. The classic shape of the liturgical year cannot be reconfigured to accommodate by explicit reference all the worthy topical issues that claim our attention today. However, just as the church's traditional Marian feasts can provoke in our day renewed appreciation for the dignity, worth, and spiritual charism of women, so also a traditional locus of observance should be sought to embody the abstract principle of ecological reverence. At one time, and in societies more pervasively agricultural than ours, rituals tied to the three Rogation Days before Ascension held promise for development in this direction.

---

7. Such a claim is made, for example, on the web site of the nonprofit EarthDay Network, online: http://www.earthday.net/about/. It's fair to wonder, though, whether the New Year on January 1, despite differences in global calendars, might be celebrated by even more people.

That is not so apparent today, despite renewed attention to Rogation Days in some quarters. In a number of faith communities, commemorations of Saint Francis of Assisi, centered ritually on animal blessings, have become the focal point for rituals acknowledging the holiness of creation. Yet the forms of this observance, which commonly falls on or near Francis's day of commemoration on October 4, vary widely.

As the root sense of "holiday" suggests, the idea of setting certain "holy" days aside from normal business derives from religious tradition. This lineage can be discerned, somewhere beneath the surface, even in the case of secular observances in our civil society. By the same token, Christian festivals trace part of their lineage not only to Hebrew rituals and festivals, but further back as well to those harvest festivals of archaic origin that preceded Jewish observances. Easter, for example, has evident antecedents in Pesach, an occasion of historical anamnesis, or recollection, that recalls in turn spring fertility and agricultural rites. With Earth Day, then, the pattern seems to have come full circle. This "holiday" carries a moral idealism reminiscent of faith-based rituals but was initiated as a secular occasion—suggesting the latter-day recovery, perhaps, of a pre-Christian rite of nature.

In any case, the broad appeal exercised by Earth Day challenges faith communities to identify a specific festival day that would celebrate the holiness of creation. For Christians, at least, such a day might best be linked to a pre-existing tradition of observance and to an episode or theme in the life of Christ. It should highlight some joyful, visionary strain of salvation history. The Transfiguration fulfills all these conditions.

How, then, might the "green" potential of this feast be accentuated? If one accepts the premise that topical novelties are, for the most part, to be avoided in liturgical renewal, a few modest changes could be implemented toward achieving this end. With benefit of the calendar adjustment already discussed, the day could be more prominently featured within a local community's cycle of yearly events. Its liturgical observance could be linked to other attractions, such as a parish fair, supper, or offbeat activities comparable to those now practiced on the April 22 Earth Day. Prior notices of the day, as well as preaching at its main liturgy, could highlight its expansive, eco-spiritual implications. Minor additions to collects and intercessory prayers would reinforce this emphasis. It would be particularly valuable to revive the custom, which survives in the Eastern Church and in pockets of Roman Catholicism, of concluding the Transfiguration liturgy with a blessing of grapes or other fruit.[8]

This physical gesture of blessing the fruit underscores the earthy, organic aspects of the feast. As such, it amplifies the sense of Eucharistic thanks for natural creation already enacted through bread and wine. And, of course, the material substance of wine is itself a spirited, transfigured product of the grape harvest. The folk custom of blessing and distributing fruit also coincides with the theme of seasonal harvest, as reinforced by the feast's commemoration in late summer. The evangelists' mention of booths or tabernacles on the mount of transfiguration also recalls the Jewish feast of Sukkot, with its further incorporation of autumn harvest festivals and thanksgiving. It remains unclear how directly this backdrop of the Feast of Tabernacles may have influenced either the gospel writers or subsequent development of the Feast of Transfiguration.[9] Nonetheless, more than one aspect of this major Jewish festival is relevant to a celebration of earth day. As classically observed, Sukkot involves something like a camping-out ritual, because during the seven-day day interval of its celebration the faithful are encouraged to stay in tent-like enclosures, living on closer rustic terms with nature by way of recollecting their ancestors' years of unsettled wandering in the wilderness. These booths were and are often constructed of palm branches. By the same token, palm trees figure plainly in the famous, sixth-century mosaic treatment of the Transfiguration in the Basilica of St. Apollinarus near Ravenna as well as in other visual representations.

There is ample precedent in church history for incorporating certain archaic "pagan" practices, as well as established Jewish practices, into Christian worship. What's more, lesser-known worship customs already associated with the Transfiguration offer ways in which the "Earth Day" potential of this feast might, without violence to tradition, be fruitfully expanded to address contemporary needs.

---

8. According to the original *Catholic Encyclopedia*, in an article titled "The Feast of the Transfiguration of Christ," the Pope also uses new wine or presses a bunch of ripe grapes into the chalice, 15:19. But this practice is not, so far as I know, otherwise part of Roman Catholic observance.

9. See Andreopoulos, *Metamorphosis*, 46, 57–60, 87–88; Heil, *The Transfiguration*, 116–18; Lee, *Transfiguration*, 19, 49, 75; and Ramsey, *The Glory of God*, 103.

AVAILABLE TEXTS AND HYMNODY FOR
TRANSFIGURATION LITURGIES

As one might expect, liturgical prayer in the Eastern Church presents an unusually rich exposure to broader themes of Transfiguration, including cosmic repercussions of the feast. Such Orthodox texts dramatize what it means to rediscover the world as divine milieu, as a meta-sacrament and source of Eucharistic joy. Words sung during the Orthodox Small Vespers for the Transfiguration declare, for instance, that Christ's shining "as lightning with glory upon the mountain" has "filled the world with light." Texts for Matins on August 6 reiterate that God's transformative illumination lights and sanctifies "the whole creation," so that "Today all things are filled with joy." The faithful are exhorted to ascend the "holy and heavenly mountain" to "stand in spirit in the city of the living God," there to be "made . . . godlike" and to behold inwardly the divine beauty that shines from Christ.[10] Yet another suggestion of the encompassing vision of Transfiguration sustained in Eastern Orthodoxy may be found in the custom of blessing grapes at the close of the day's central liturgy. Although this gesture obviously derives from summer harvest rituals, it also seems to carry associations with Eucharistic fruits of the vine and, in turn, with renewal of the whole natural creation.

Even in Western churches, current liturgical materials offer a fair opportunity for preachers to help their congregations appreciate just why the Transfiguration matters. Thus, in the Episcopal Church's liturgy, the Collect by Huntington (see text at note 5) invites from the outset reflection on the feast's transcendent, mystagogical character, through its petition that "we, being delivered from the disquietude of this world, may by faith behold the King in his beauty." This regal theme is sustained into the recitation of Psalm 99, with its homage to the Lord enthroned on high who is a "lover of justice," whose presence can shake the earth, and who is worthy of worship "on his holy hill." Readings appointed for the day include, in addition to the prayerfully situated Transfiguration narrative from Luke's gospel, the story from Exodus of Moses' descent from Mount Sinai and the testimony in 2 Peter by which the author, speaking in the apostle's voice yet in solidarity with us all, affirms that "we were with him on the holy mountain." The story of Moses' close encounter with God on a mountain peak, an episode that leaves his own

10. *The Festal Menaion*, 469, 481, 494–95.

face shining with glory, offers typological promise of God's will to exalt human nature.

The *Revised Common Lectionary*, now in common use for Eucharistic worship in several denominations, designates these or similar readings for the last Sunday in Epiphany over the course of its three-year cycle. Something of the Transfiguration's more expansive application, as well as its significance as a feast of beauty, is conveyed through such texts. Psalm 50, for example (appointed for Year B), describes how the Lord "has called the earth from the rising of the sun to its setting" and how "out of Zion, perfect in its beauty, God reveals himself in glory." Psalm 27, appointed for Year B of Last Epiphany in the Episcopal Church, likewise expresses its author's heartfelt desire to "dwell in the house of the Lord all of my life; To behold the fair beauty of the Lord and to seek him in his temple."[11]

In sum, there is ample reason for the church today to renew its celebration of this ancient feast. Beyond its ecumenical links with Eastern Orthodoxy, the Transfiguration offers a spiritual wellspring the church might draw upon in confronting issues of environmental ethics and practice. A theology and liturgical spirituality of Transfiguration also promises to expand ecological vision beyond the stewardship focus that has thus claimed almost exclusive attention within mainline churches. Whereas the Church's official response to faith and environment issues now inclines toward the adoption of didactic, ethical, and bureaucratic approaches, yielding such things as convention resolutions or instructional workshops, the gospel of Transfiguration might enable her to respond in more integrally liturgical, contemplative, and doxological terms, befitting her authentic charism as the Church. For unless the Church develops these latter gifts, she risks becoming, in her environmental witness, little more than a technically incompetent adjunct of the Sierra Club.

Beyond rites that are linked explicitly to the Transfiguration, which Leo the Great described as a "great sacrament"[12] in itself, Christianity's central act of worship in the Eucharistic liturgy also deserves to be recognized as its ritual enactment of metamorphosis or transformation par excellence. A promise of universal transformation stands, as Teilhard de Chardin's prose-poem, "The Mass on the World," makes plain, behind

11. *Revised Common Lectionary*, 98; *The Book of Common Prayer*, 617.

12. McGuckin, *The Transfiguration*, 281.

the whole movement of the Eucharistic action. This action presupposes some form of change not only in the disposition of communicants, as dramatized inwardly through the progression from offertory through epiclesis and consecration, but also in the elements of bread and wine.[13]

Whether interpreted along various denominational lines as transubstantiation, consubstantiation, transignification, or something else, this "elemental" change is significant. In its agreed statement, *Baptism, Eucharist and Ministry*, the Faith and Order Commission of the World Council of Churches describes the Eucharist as "the great sacrifice of praise by which the Church speaks on behalf of the whole creation." In addition to confirming that Eucharistic action "signifies what the world is to become," this interdenominational statement identifies the sacrament's deepest reality" with the "total being of Christ who comes to us," not only "to feed us" but to "transform our entire being." The bread and produce of the vine, while understood to embody sacramentally Christ's body and blood, also represent ordinary features of material reality. Wheat and a beverage that is itself the product of a transmutation process in grapes—these things are, as *Baptism, Eucharist and Ministry* reminds us, at once "fruits of the earth and of human labour."[14] As Teilhard grasped so pointedly, transmutation of the whole material cosmos is thereby implicated in the Eucharistic action. Classic language found in the Sanctus portion of the Eucharistic canon underscores the point that the sacred action—including as it does "angels and archangels, and the whole company of heaven"—participates in a cosmic drama of transformation much larger than the circle of its human celebrants. And for the community to sing that "Heaven and earth are full of God's glory" is, in effect, to verbalize and ritualize its affirmation of what is revealed through the Transfiguration.

Finally, it is worth repeating that the celebratory aspect of Transfiguration Day, which we might recover today as a new festival of Creation, also encircles the Passion. So the scope of this sacred feast is broad indeed. The divine cloud on the mountain does not obscure, but rather, concentrates and sanctifies the afflictions of Christ and the world. And since 1945, we cannot forget that another cloud, the unholy cloud of death at Hiroshima, hangs over every commemoration of August 6. Only three years after Hiroshima, which he never mentions,

---

13. Teilhard de Chardin, "The Mass on the World," 19–37.

14. *Baptism*, 10–12.

and thirteen years before becoming Archbishop of Canterbury, Michael Ramsey concluded his study of the Transfiguration with these sober but hopeful words, which I think still speak to the desperation of our own postmodern era:

> Confronted as he is with a universe more than ever terrible in the blindness of its processes and the destructiveness of its potentialities, mankind must be led to the Christian faith not as a panacea of progress nor as an other-worldly solution unrelated to history, but as a Gospel of Transfiguration. Such a Gospel both transcends the world and speaks to the immediate here-and-now. He who is transfigured is the Son of Man; and, as He discloses on Mount Hermon another world, He reveals that no part of created things and no moment of created time lies outside the power of the Spirit, who is Lord, to change from glory into glory.[15]

15. Ramsey, *The Glory of God*, 147.

7

The Art of Transfiguration

FROM THE PATRISTIC ERA onward, the beauty manifested in and through Jesus on the mount of Transfiguration has been a prominent theme in scriptural commentaries. Gregory of Nazianzen, for example, read the evangelists' account in light of Psalm 45:3, arguing that the transfigured one is here seen to be "'gracious and beautiful beyond the sons of men'" as "he flashed like lightning on the mountain and became brighter than the sun, intimating mysteries of the age to come." A comparable invocation of Psalm 45 appears in liturgical texts for the feast day of August 6. Besides Gregory, a number of other Greek fathers—including Maximus the Confessor, Basil of Caesarea, and John of Damascus—were drawn to elaborate on this theme. Maximus believed that because the Transfiguration allowed Jesus' disciples to "know the Logos in the flesh," it led them "to see his glory and to understand that he 'was beautiful beyond the sons of men.'" For John of Damascus, the episode revealed as well the divinely imaged beauty of human nature itself. The comeliness of Jesus' face and garments on the mountain, in contrast to the disfigurement he endured in his passion, is likewise a familiar theme in commentaries by Latin fathers such as Leo I and Gregory the Great.[1]

Iconic portrayals often reinforce the point. Dazzling light, shining from Jesus' face and garments, reveals not only divine glory but an all-surpassing loveliness that his disciples had never recognized before. From this standpoint beauty is, in fact, closely allied to "glory," a term that in both Hebrew (*kabod*) and Greek (*doxa*) scriptural usage implies disclosure of a divine radiance of form. No other episode in the New Testament highlights the *beauty* of God more memorably than the Transfiguration—so far, at least, as exegetical tradition has construed the relevant texts.

1. McGuckin, *The Transfiguration*, esp. 171, 169, 198–9, 203.

Christian theology has not always held aesthetics in high regard. In some quarters, the attribute of divine beauty has been regarded as suspect or trivial by comparison with theologies emphasizing God's righteousness, love, faithfulness, transcendence, or power.

If one's personal discovery of justification and salvation is taken to be the sine qua non of faith, aesthetic dimensions of the sacred may be dismissed as purely ornamental. The religious significance of beauty has often been acknowledged, though, in Christian faith traditions disposed to adopt a broadly sacramental and incarnational view of life. Theological aesthetics plays a central role, for example, in writings of Hans Urs von Balthasar, a noted Roman Catholic Swiss theologian. The holiness of beauty is everywhere presumed in literary works such as Dante's *Divine Comedy* or Milton's *Paradise Lost*; in the colorful artistry of Eastern Orthodox icons; and in the formulations of theologians ranging from Thomas Aquinas to John Calvin, along with New England Calvinists such as Jonathan Edwards and Edward Taylor.

All of these witnesses agree that if conformity with the divine will— a harmony with Being itself—is the essence of Christian living, then the very idea of moral virtue can scarcely be divorced from beauty. Right living is itself an art of the highest order. Moreover, the doctrine of God as Holy Trinity, like that of Christ as divine Logos, implies recognition of a beauteous order, harmony, and proportion at the heart of existence.

No wonder Von Balthasar wrote that one who disdains the name of beauty "as if she were the ornament of a bourgeois past . . . can no longer pray and soon will no longer be able to love."[2] Richard Harries, who has likewise pondered the conjunction between ethics and aesthetics, or between the beauty of God and the beauty of the world, claims that "without a positive theological evaluation of beauty there is no motive to delight in God and no compelling reason to love him." And he cites Simone Weil, to the effect that "'The beauty of the world is Christ's tender smile for us coming through matter like a sacrament.'"[3]

Thus, there is considerable support from ancient and modern tradition for the conclusion that literature, art, music, and architecture carry religious significance—both in general and with particular reference to representations of the Transfiguration.

As our primary exposure to the Transfiguration gospel derives from scriptural texts, literary expansions on this theme are the most obvious

2. Von Balthasar, *The Glory*, 1:18.

3. Harries, *Art*, 6, 35.

form of artistry inspired by metamorphosis. Such artistry receives much attention throughout this book. Two other modes of artistic reflection that warrant discrete recognition here, though, are music and iconography.

Because music is a kinetic art form well suited to dramatizing transformation within time, the theme of metamorphosis finds at least generalized expression in several specimens of aural composition. Music, by its very nature, embodies a process of dynamic change—rather than a still-life portrait. In programmatic or vocalized compositions, some shift or metamorphosis in thematic material may be demonstrated as well. Richard Strauss's tone poem on "Death and Transfiguration" (*Tod und Verklärung*, 1888–89) offers a case in point. According to the composer, it portrays the last hours of a dying man who faces a final crisis as he recalls the course of his life journey and the failure to realize his high ideals. Though the work reaches a triumphant conclusion, gathered in a hymnlike theme first voiced by brass and woodwinds, Strauss's non-Christian sense of this metamorphosis was tied only loosely to gospel principles. In Strauss's view, the protagonist's transformational apotheosis crowns a process that combines something of Stoic resignation with a quasi-Platonic and mystical—but not particularly theistic—faith in the soul's immortality. Perhaps the composer, still a young man at the time he wrote *Tod und Verklärung*, also imagined that he might, through his own musical artistry, hope to transform and transcend the fearful consequences of mortality.

I know of only one musical work, however, that explores at length the deeply evocative meaning of Christian Transfiguration through sound as well as vocalized texts. Composed by Olivier Messiaen between 1965 and 1969, this work bears the straightforward title of *La Transfiguration de Notre Seigneur Jésus-Christ* (The Transfiguration of our Lord Jesus Christ).

Unfortunately, *La Transfiguration* is rarely performed. Like most of those who might be curious to encounter the piece, I have thus far been able to hear it only in recording. It is scored for a formidable array of vocalists and instrumentalists. In its final form, it calls for the services of seven instrumental soloists, tenor and baritone leads, mixed choir, and a large orchestra. Drawing on a rich span of musical coloration and modal textures, the composer exploits several percussion instruments to dramatic effect. The work's structure is mystically aligned to present a sevenfold ordering of reflections, with its two-part sequence numbering seven movements in each part. A symmetrical pattern of structure and musical motifs connects the two septenaries. Each septenary concludes with a majestic chorale in blocked chords. *La Transfiguration* also manifests Messiaen's characteristic fascination with birdsong. The aviary splendor evoked here includes instrumental representation of more than seventy species, representing creatures from diverse ecosystems and continents. The composer's invocation of birdlife ranges from the cries of mountain birds, such as the peregrine falcon and Bonelli's Eagle, to musical counterparts of the vibrantly colored eastern bluebird and rock thrush.

That the Transfiguration affects not only the appearance of Jesus but the atmosphere in which we perceive the whole of creation is a point amplified by Messiaen's insistence on the sacred beauty of birds. Birds enrich his plan of composition in several ways. Most obviously, their music—represented so as to blend nature with art—contributes aurally to the vibrant, energetic mood sustained through much of this work. Within the carefully structured artistry of *La Transfiguration*, representation of the disparate sounds and motions of these creatures suggests a wild, free-flowing vitality.

Thematically, too, birds suggest qualities of elevation and transcendence suited to the idea of Transfiguration. That the Holy Spirit is commonly pictured as a dove[4] is relevant here, too, insofar as exegetical tradition confirms the Spirit's presence—in and beyond the overshadowing cloud—at the Transfiguration. At the same time, Messiaen's attention to scores of distinct bird species reminds us of the creaturely particularity of nature, a sensuous splendor that is also celebrated at and through the Transfiguration. As Harries observes, "Beauty is the product of honest attention to the particular."[5]

The Latin texts Messiaen selected for vocalization in *La Transfiguration* include biblical selections from the Vulgate version of Matthew's gospel, Paul's epistles, selected psalms, Genesis, and the Book of Wisdom, together with reflective commentary from Thomas Aquinas. Throughout this monumental work, the composer makes extensive use of woodwinds to voice the birdsongs and supply musical coloration; he also relies heavily on percussive instruments to heighten impressions of the numinous and to mark dramatic pauses. Thus, the opening sequence of

4. Implications of such bird-God symbolism are discussed by Wallace, *Finding God*, 9, 22, 41–3, 50–56.

5. Harries, *Art*, 12.

choral chant from Matthew's gospel narrative is punctuated by sounding of cymbals, gongs, liturgical-sounding bells, and a telling hiatus just before the enunciation of "et transfiguratus est ante eos" (and he was transfigured before them). Fearful dimensions of the mountaintop episode are emphasized in the setting of passages such as the liturgically familiar allusion to earth-shaking lightning in Psalm 77 (section 3 of the composition) and the reference in Genesis 28:17 to a place of holy dread (section 12).[6]

Yet Messiaen's work as a whole acknowledges that the Transfiguration is a sacred mystery encompassing several layers of meaning. Other sections of his composition stress the beauty and splendor of the "eternal light" (*lucis aeternae*), the grace of affiliation as adoptive children of God, the future radiance of God's saints, or the joy of discovering on earth a distinct physical locus for God's divine presence. This last point is underscored through the voicing of texts such as those describing the psalmist's satisfaction at dwelling in the Lord's tabernacles (Ps 84:1–3). The first septenary ends with a "chorale of the Holy Mountain," sung in solemn homophony, that offers praise "in the city of our God" on "his holy mountain" (Ps 48:1); the second with a grander yet "Chorale of the Glorious Light," keyed to Psalm 26:8: "I have loved the habitation of thy house and the place where thine honour dwelleth." Moreover, the composer discloses elsewhere that his appreciation of the place-specific, mountain grandeur in the gospel account had been enlarged by personal experience. In an explanatory commentary, he relates the sublime radiance and holy terror he portrays in section 12 of the composition to the striking impressions of sunlight and snow he had once received while gazing on Mount Blanc with its surrounding peaks and glaciers. This same section includes several birdsongs mimicked instrumentally, as well as a cello solo—played in the premier performance by Mistilov Rostropovich—that the composer imagined as singing out "the simple clarity of eternal light."

Through the innovative scoring of *La Transfiguration*, Messiaen creates a vast span of aural impressions—ranging from the stern solidity of deep-voiced trombones and bass vocalists to surreal glissandos from

---

6. I have consulted and cited from vocal texts of this work as they appear, together with remarks from Messiaen, in liner notes accompanying the 1994 CD recording with Reinbert de Leeuw and the Netherlands Radio Symphony Orchestra (Auvidis Montaigne label). For accounts of the genesis, performing history, and general character of *La Transfiguration*, see Dingle, *The Life of Messiaen*, 168–74; and Hill and Simeone, *Messiaen*, 263–73, 293.

the strings and a mélange of treble, agitated woodwind sounds interspersed with startling outbursts from the percussion section. The overall effect, particularly by virtue of the birdsong invocations, is to dramatize the Transfiguration's significance as a transhistorical phenomenon permeating the whole of creation.

Musical works not directly inspired by orthodox religious ideas or texts can also deepen one's appreciation of a spirituality centered in metamorphosis. For me, full-scale compositions that particularly invite consideration in this light include the *Ein Deustches Requiem* (*German Requiem*) of Johannes Brahms together with the Second Symphony (known as the Resurrection) and the monumental Third Symphony of Gustav Mahler. In Brahms's *German Requiem*, for example, processes of transformation are played out in several ways. Most explicitly, the work bespeaks metamorphosis in the text chosen for the sixth of its seven sections. There a solo voice intones Paul's declaration in 1 Corinthians 15:51 that "we shall all be changed" (*wir warden aber alle verwandelt warden*).

Larger patterns of transformation can also be discerned in the process by which this requiem engages us imaginatively in a confrontation with human mortality. Toward the opening, Brahms centers attention on the implacable fact of death, the fleeting character of all life on earth. A somber and unison choral declamation, set against tympani strokes suggesting a death knell or heartbeat, reminds us that "all flesh is as grass," while a subsequent baritone solo ponders the need to reflect on "my end and the measure of my days." Following the death of his mother, Brahms added a section with a soprano solo (section 5) that combines a heartfelt exposition of grief with a reminder of God's maternal solace. To what extent the composer was inspired to write this work to mourn his mother, the death of his dear friend Robert Schumann, or other circumstances of loss remains uncertain. But whatever personal occasions of grief informed his composition at various stages, the work doubtless aims to encompass the totality of human sorrow—as befits its alternative title, *A Human Requiem*, which was also consistent with his intent.[7]

In the metamorphosis of mourning that *Ein Deustches Requiem* enacts, consolation is not only expressed through the art of music but also defined and discovered in relation to aesthetics. Two textual motifs—one from the Beatitudes, another introduced with parallel phrasing—frame the work as a whole. Beginning with a sotto voce pronouncement from

7. For a general description of this work's background and character, see Steinberg, *Choral Masterworks*, 68–76.

the chorus of the blessedness of "those who mourn," Brahms shifts our attention to the blessedness of the dead by the time we reach his concluding choral declamation. Along the way, though the composer never invokes texts that mention Christ or redemption, he does cite Paul's confidence in a post-mortem transformation as well as the psalmist's yearning to dwell perpetually in the Lord's tabernacles. Despite Brahms's expressed inclination toward agnosticism, his composition transcends that personal disposition to expose an eschatological hope. Moreover, its concluding choral text from the Book of Revelation combines a beatitude-like reference to the blessed rest of the deceased with an affirmation that their works "do follow them." A person's deeds somehow endure, albeit in ways unfathomable, beyond his or her appointed lifespan. Such has indeed been the case with Brahms's own masterpiece, which enjoys renewed life with each performance.

What a poignantly consoling thought for a composer who knew that before long he, too, must join the ranks of the deceased! Plainly, the power of this requiem has endured beyond Brahms's lifetime, so that even for nonbelievers, the work itself enacts artistically that very metamorphosis of death suggested thematically by its texts. Similarly, in *Four Quartets*, T. S. Eliot reflects on the paradoxical truth that while "Words move, music moves / Only in time,"[8] such temporal words, music, and images can also reach toward timelessness.

In the case of music, art's engagement with the elasticity of time has become all the more evident with the development of modern recording technology. Most of the performers—including conductor Otto Klemperer and soprano soloist Elisabeth Schwarzkopf—whose "works follow them" in a cherished recording I own of the *German Requiem* have died since this recording was made in 1962. I find it sobering to recall this fact and to recognize that they themselves are now at rest from their labors, even as I hear them perform so vibrantly, again and again, this work whose subject is death and mourning. At least one version of death's metamorphosis is already apparent in the works of artistry preserved on such recordings. But do all of our works follow us, or might we dare to imagine even our failings transfigured in death? Should it matter to us now, when we hear again the surpassing loveliness of Schwarzkopf's voice, that this German-born artist had once been a member and supporter of the Nazi party? Or is it only the beauty of her art and best self that endures? God only knows.

8. Eliot, *Four Quartets*, 121.

Certainly, though, icons are a form of sacred art that has long offered enduring access to the mystery of the Transfiguration. As Archbishop Rowan Williams points out, "the Eastern Christian representation of this event has been much the same for nearly a thousand years."[9] And the Transfiguration as a "supremely *visual* event"[10] has long remained a favored subject of iconographers in the Eastern Church. Such images are not intended to satisfy usual purposes of artistic expression or production. From the standpoint of Byzantine orthodoxy, icons invite veneration, not artistic appreciation, because they offer nothing less than a visual parallel of the Scriptures.[11] Modern commentary on the theology and spirituality of icons has already given just attention to treatments of the Transfiguration.[12] I wish to add here only a few reflections on two among the many celebrated mosaic and iconic representations.

Figure 3

One of these is the sixth-century apse mosaic preserved in St. Catherine's Monastery at Mount Sinai (see fig. 3). This very early treatment differs from most subsequent visualizations in its placement of

9. Williams, *The Dwelling*, 3.

10. Andreopoulos, *Metamorphosis*, 13.

11. Ibid., 11.

12. Such treatments, in addition to those of Andreopoulos and Williams, include those of Hart, *The Icon*; and Ouspensky and Lossky, *The Meaning*, 209–12.

the disciples. Whereas later renderings usually show Peter on the left, James on the right, and John in the middle, the Saint Catherine version situates Peter directly below Christ along a vertical axis. It is fitting that Peter should be depicted here as prostrate with wonder before the theophany that he finds blazing unexpectedly on Mount Tabor. For the theophany that Moses had experienced from the burning bush on Mount Sinai, where this image is displayed in St. Catherine's Monastery, likewise involved an effusion of light and energy. That the one mountain theophany is typologically linked to the second, wherein Moses also appears, could scarcely be declared more plainly. It is also telling that a luminescent emblem of the cross should have been placed here above Christ and Peter. Three sacred mountains—Sinai, Tabor, and Calvary—are effectually conjoined in the theological span of this image. As Andreas Andreopoulos points out, the threefold depiction of Moses in panels above the Transfiguration also carries theological significance within the larger composition.[13]

Similarly, the mosaic initiates a doubled pattern of triformal representation—with the lower triptych of John, Peter, and James paralleled in the semicircular arrangement of Moses, Jesus, and Elijah. In addition to rays marking the vertical axis, a trinitarian pattern is further suggested here by three beams of light projected toward the left and another three toward the right.

The Saint Catherine mosaic is noteworthy, too, insofar as it offers the earliest extant example of an oval mandorla. The mandorla, a conventional framing device drawn around Christ's body, symbolizes a distinctive concentration of divine glory. Moreover, the mandorla found at Sinai, with its three concentric layers of coloration running from blue to black, may reflect not only a model of mystical ascent, but also the deep texture of concentric spheres enclosing the entire universe. This cosmic symbolism is strengthened in the case of the oval mandorla by the archetypal and regenerative implications of the egg-shaped pattern.[14] In fact, the Sinai mosaic enlarges our sense of an all-encompassing, cosmic egg by juxtaposing the vertical mandorla that surrounds Christ with a horizontal, egg-shaped pattern that encloses the larger tableau. The perpendicular

13. Andreopoulos, *Metamorphosis*, 127–39, esp. 131–2; Lane also presents a comparative account of Sinai and Tabor mountain symbolism, based on visits to both sites, in *The Solace*, 124–47.

14. Andreopoulos, *Metamorphosis*, 90–91, 136–7, 145–54.

symmetry of this design is further aligned with the full compass reach suggested by those equally extended arms of the cross set above the scene. Already by the time of Justinian's reign in the sixth century, the artistry of this work shows a well-developed appreciation of the Transfiguration's opening toward a universal vision of space and time.

A comparable depth and expanse of vision is expressed, through quite different visual techniques, in a famous Novgorod icon from the late fifteenth century. The Saint Catherine mosaic, perhaps because it is itself set on Mount Sinai, lacks visualization of the Transfiguration's mountainous setting. By contrast, the Novgorod icon (fig. 2) shows a materially textured landscape strewn with rocks and plants. The serenity represented in the icon's upper triptych complements the craggy disorder and angularity that enfolds the lower portion's trio of disciples. This icon is entrancing in several respects—by virtue, for example, of the rounded grace with which it portrays Moses and Elijah engaged in conversing with Jesus. Insofar as the image captures a moment suspended within but distinct from ordinary time, the sense it conveys of weightless elevation on the part of Moses, Jesus, and Elijah seems appropriate.

Yet the icon's most compelling feature, I think, lies in the contour of its mandorla. Round rather than oval, this mandorla follows customary patterns in its layered distribution of shadings. This ordering of concentric spaces corresponds to the representation of a cosmic expanse across the heavens in other Byzantine icons. From a black disk in the center, the viewer's eye moves outward toward three other spheres of coloration, each progressively lighter. But this icon's distinctive design, including its placement of thin rays of gold, also conveys something more. The mandorla is configured here to offer the appearance of a great eye.

What might be signified by this ocular presence within the sacred tableau? One likely association the figure bears is with the "Great Eye of God" that iconographers, by venerable tradition, would have painted as the starting point of their divine exercise. As Andreopoulos describes this practice, "the first thing ancient iconographers did as they started an icon—after days of prayer and fasting—was to paint a great eye on the empty canvas and write the word 'God' underneath."[15] The ocular shaping of the Novgorod mandorla, with Christ at its center, apparently overlays this custom. And the dark core of this eye, reminiscent of a pupil, remains inscrutable and impenetrable. To gaze upon this image is, in effect, to

15. Ibid., 27, 252.

encounter God's dynamic, personal presence as the all-seeing eye gazes upon—and, in effect, pierces through—the viewer. Even as you look, you sense that Someone is looking at you. Such art is not to be regarded as mere artifact, to be studied or manipulated with objective detachment.

It is fitting, then, to recognize this eye that contains the Transfigured Christ as the great eye of God. But I think it fair to say that it also reflects the eye of the viewer. From the human side, the eye is a portal opening toward unfathomable depths of reality. We simultaneously see and are seen. Such, in fact, is the character of all encounter with a living and personal God. The Transfiguration is, by its very nature, an intersubjective phenomenon. In the transfigurative experience, it is not only *what* one perceives but also *how* one perceives Christ and the world that undergoes transformation.

Saint Paul likewise affirmed that in learning to see Christ, we as subjects learn to internalize what we would otherwise have construed to be merely the object of faith. The division we typically experience between ourselves as subject and objects of our perception starts to dissolve, as "all of us, with unveiled faces, seeing the glory of the Lord as though reflected in a mirror, are being transformed into the same image from one degree of glory to another" (2 Cor 3:18). In the process, "our inner nature is being renewed day by day" (2 Cor 4:16). In the circular outline of its great eye, the Novgorod mandorla likewise reflects divine attributes of eternity and perfection.

The great eye embedded in this icon is at once inspiring and somewhat unsettling. In this respect it accords with gospel descriptions of the Transfiguration. It accords, for that matter, with the metamorphic principle inherent in all artistic endeavor. The creation of art always demands some transmutation of material form, as spirit acts through human agency to shape from that form or substance a new thing. Insofar as all art involves, in some measure, a metamorphosis of natural elements requiring the destruction of what preceded its creation, it can be threatening by nature. But it is also, perhaps still more essentially, hopeful—insofar as it affirms that change happens, that there can indeed be something new under the sun. The iconographer who painted the Novgorod icon doubtless saw the Christ of Transfiguration conjoined with the enthroned one who declares, in the closing book of Scripture, "See, I am making all things new" (Rev 21:5). And learning to see the world with new eyes opens the way to beholding Beauty itself.

8

Transforming Society

ONE REASON, PERHAPS, WHY a mystical outlook centered in the Transfiguration receives little notice in churches today is that any such spirituality falls under suspicion as esoteric and escapist. Even if one managed to share something of the ecstatic, visionary experience attributed to the apostles on Mount Tabor, might not the aspiration to sustain such a realization become self-serving? For that matter, isn't the mystical pursuit of inner peace and satisfaction simply an evasion, a retreat from larger social realities? Is it really consistent with Christian charity to flee ordinary life in the world for the sake of pursuing a contemplative life or savoring a mountaintop experience, when so many challenges and calls to active service await us in communities down below?

Such complaints have long been lodged against those committed to contemplative monasticism and, more broadly, against all exponents of the mystical way. These suspicions strike me as largely ill-founded. Granted, much that is advertised today under the heading of "spirituality" involves techniques for satisfying some sort of individualistic pleasure principle. Yet the master guides of Christian spirituality have traditionally taught disciples how to embrace an interior life conjoined with God—and by extension, with the whole communion of saints. The mystical response to grace thus represents not an escape from reality, but progress toward fulfilling a vision centered in the ultimate reality of God.

Thomas Merton, for example, underscores the point that meditation and contemplation have traditionally been known to expand one's "capacity to understand and serve others." Deep interior awareness should heighten rather than obscure sensitivity to "urgent needs of the time." Contemplation is properly antecedent to right action in the world since "he who attempts to act and do things for others or for the world without deepening his own self-understanding, freedom, integrity and capacity to love, will not have anything to give others."[1] Evelyn Underhill points out that a mystical passion for transformation is what led "St. Catherine of Siena from contemplation to politics; Joan of Arc to the salvation of France . . . Florence Nightingale to battle with officials, vermin, dirt, and disease in the soldiers' hospitals; Octavia Hill to make in London slums something a little nearer 'the shadows of the angels' houses' than that which the practical landlord usually provides."[2]

With more particular reference to the gospel story of Transfiguration, spirit-motivated prophets of social change, such as Archbishop Desmond Tutu and peace activist John Dear, emphasize not so much the moment of transcendent illumination as its consequences. Peter, James, and John visited only briefly on the mountain summit before descending to face once more the burdens of ordinary life in the world. And the social order to which they returned surely needed—and still needs—metamorphosis. For social reform to become imaginable, one must be sustained by some loftier vision and by hope for the possibility of change.

In his book titled *God Has a Dream: A Vision of Hope for Our Time*, Archbishop Desmond Tutu enlarges on this principle. He describes in quite personal terms how his involvement in South Africa's anti-apartheid struggle was grounded in Christian faith—above all, in a faith-based hope of transformation epitomized by the Transfiguration gospel. Such, in fact, emerges here as Tutu's defining "vision of hope for our time."

Just as Tutu believes that South Africa's first open presidential election became collectively for its citizens "a deeply spiritual event, a religious experience, a transfiguration experience," so also he identifies his personal recovery of hope with a Transfiguration episode that he recalls taking place for him as he sat in a priory garden during a season of discouragement. Gazing there at a stark wooden cross set amid pale winter grass, he felt weighed down, disheartened by the indignities his compatriots were suffering during the apartheid era. South Africa looked indeed like "a hopeless case if ever there was one." Yet his mood changed when he recalled that this brown vegetation would, within a few weeks, turn to lush greenery. For Tutu, this metamorphosis within the natural order prefigured humanity's hope for social and universal transformation, even within the apparently hopeless circumstance of South African politics. Moreover, he discloses that this episode, wherein

1. Merton, *Contemplation*, 155, 160.
2. Underhill, *Practical Mysticism*, 128.

he felt his faith renewed, took place on the Feast of the Transfiguration.[3] That circumstance can scarcely be coincidental. He explains,

> As I sat quietly in the garden I realized the power of transfiguration—of God's transformation—in our world. The principle of transfiguration is at work when something so unlikely as the brown grass that covers our veld in winter becomes bright green again. Or when the tree with gnarled leafless branches bursts forth with the sap flowing so that the birds sit chirping in the leafy branches. Or when the once dry streams gurgle with swift flowing water. When winter gives way to spring and nature seems to experience its own resurrection.
>
> The principle of transfiguration says nothing, no one and no situation, is "untransfigurable," that the whole of creation, nature, waits expectantly for its transfiguration, when it will be released from its bondage and share in the glorious liberty of the children of God, when it will not be just dry inert matter but will be translucent with divine glory.[4]

Potentially, at least, if we view human beings through eyes of faith, the glorious dignity of each person should appear luminescent. Archbishop Tutu suggests that Buddhists, who are apt to bow reverentially when greeting another by way of recognizing this dignity, have the right idea. For him, it is only a "spirituality of transformation," centered in the vision of a transfigured world, that has enabled him and other seekers of God's shalom to endure amid woes such as apartheid, war, and the persistence of poverty and disease. He testifies that it is the contemplative, serene, and centering force represented in the Transfiguration that has inspired him to pursue peace and social reform. Tutu insists that "this authentic spirituality of transformation is the basis for any true and lasting transfiguration in our world." Long committed to sustaining a serious prayer life, he affirms, "Discovering God's stillness, hearing God's voice, is not, as I have said, the luxury of a few contemplatives. It is the basis for real peace and real justice."[5]

Another recurrent theme throughout Archbishop Tutu's reflections is the need for human beings to assume their proper role as God's partners in the project of metamorphosis. The scriptural display of glory on that high mountain is not simply a prediction, to be received passively,

3. Tutu, *God Has a Dream*, 7, 125.

4. Ibid., 3.

5. Ibid., 108–9.

but a call to active participation. Accordingly, he insists that "We are the agents of transformation that God uses to transfigure His world."[6] Nonetheless, a proper response to that call demands humility and a deep apprehension of grace—a trust in power beyond oneself. Much of what passes for social revolution may, after all, amount only to a transfer of power from one group to another, not a transformation of power. Tutu points out that "Jesus tried to propagate a new paradigm of power," in which power corresponds not to someone's force of rule but to a capacity "for being compassionate . . . for being the servant of all."[7] Transforming the character and definition of power in accord with spiritual convictions is far more challenging than achieving a transfer of hegemony from one class or group to another. Yet some such metamorphosis of Realpolitik is precisely what the Truth and Reconciliation Commission sought to encourage in South Africa—sought and largely achieved.

For John Dear, too, Jesus' ascent of Mount Tabor with his three friends represents a radical departure from the world's usual ways of violence and unjust privilege. Like other mountain episodes recounted both within and beyond Judeo-Christian tradition, this ascent of the mountain of God opens a way toward envisioning that loftier perspective on reality that accords with Jesus' vision of contemplative nonviolence. To journey thus in faith with Jesus and to share his vision would mean trying "to see the world, yourself, your family and friends, and the whole human race from God's perspective, through the eyes of unconditional love and infinite compassion."[8] Dear contends that a journey of faith also demands, contrary to Peter's wish, a willingness to descend from satisfactions available at the summit to labor below toward fulfilling Jesus' mission in the world.

For Dear, then, the "mountaintop grace" of the Transfiguration is directly relevant to the involvement of present-day disciples in global issues—above all, in the imperative to foster world peace. He insists that "The story of the Transfiguration is not a pious myth reserved for a few religious fanatics or Scripture scholars. Set against the frightening reality of today's wars, nuclear weapons and global violence, it is a last-ditch call from the God of peace to adopt Jesus' spirituality of nonviolence and to

6. Ibid., 15.

7. Ibid., 121.

8. Dear, *Transfiguration*, 35.

reject our potential for total nuclear destruction once and for all."[9] Dear finds special inspiration for his call to bear witness as a peace activist and champion of disarmament—so as to endure arrest, disdain, and discomfort along the way—in the story of Mount Tabor, a place he has known well by reflection and through personal pilgrimage. For him, Tabor is spiritually bound not only to sites as disparate as Sinai, Mount Rainier, Los Alamos, and Hiroshima, but also to modern heroes of the faith, such as Martin Luther King, Jr., Dorothy Day, and Oscar Romero.

Dear's exhortation to share in God's transformation of society extends well beyond antimilitarism, however. His book also calls for wholehearted allegiance to Jesus' proclamation of a genuinely new world order. He writes,

> If we want to live an authentic, faith-filled life, we need to proclaim good news to the poor, liberty to prisoners, vision to the blind, liberation to the oppressed, the cancellation of the Third World debt, and the redistribution of the world's resources from the First World nations to the poorer nations, so that everyone on the planet will have food, shelter, health care, education, employment, and dignity. This is the work of Jesus. Because we are his followers, it is our work too. It will get us in trouble and lead us one day to the mountain of God in search of solitude, charity, guidance, and peace.[10]

The radical personal witness of Dear, a Jesuit priest known for displaying nonviolent resistance to war and to nuclear stockpiling, recalls the civil disobedience practiced by other American Jesuits around the time of the Vietnam War. To be sure, his exclusive endorsement of pacifism as *the* Christian standard of war policy in the realm of social ethics is hard for many to accept, much less to practice. But one can scarcely dismiss his impassioned argument that transformation in Christ demands this much. With respect to that argument, two points in Dear's exegesis of the Mount Tabor narrative strike me as freshly provocative. First, he contends that it is lack of faith that leads us to discount the Transfiguration as nothing more than fanciful poetry or naïve idealism. "If we had the courage—the faith!—to take the text seriously," he insists, "the world would be disarmed, transformed, and transfigured," as would "each one of us." Yet fear, timidity, and incredulity cause us to

9. Ibid., 172.
10. Ibid., 23.

block out the vision—in effect, to "sleep through the presence and glory of God,"[11] just as Luke describes Jesus' disciples doing on the mountain of transformation.

Dear raises another salient point of exegesis in his remarks about the conclusion of Matthew's gospel. Matthew informs us that the resurrected Lord had arranged to meet his followers again in Galilee and, more specifically, on "the mountain to which Jesus had directed them" (Matt 28:16). Might it not be fair to surmise that this mountain, where Jesus delivers the commission to "make disciples of all nations," is none other than that upon which the inner circle had seen him transfigured? If so, the larger story dramatizes all the more that personal transformation during temporary removal *from* the social world issues in a transformative mission *to* the world.

The literary testimony of Harriet Beecher Stowe further illustrates how, in the light of transfigurative spirituality, reform movements can become something more than programs to engineer social improvement. For Stowe, eliminating the scourge of chattel slavery was the crucial challenge facing nineteenth-century America. As an evangelical Christian, she regarded slavery not merely as a social ill or political aggravation to be remedied by degrees. In *Uncle Tom's Cabin*, she sought to convince readers that slavery was sin—and, therefore, absolutely intolerable. Insofar as sin involves division, separation from God, and alienation from one's better self, Stowe regarded slavery as the very quintessence of sin. Immediate emancipation thus became for her a moral imperative. The original sin of American slavery not only divided slave families but also separated free citizens from their God, a God whose wrath and justice Stowe feared would bring cataclysm unless the nation repented speedily. For Stowe, two different but affiliated orders of personal conversion were needed to avoid national peril: religious conversion of heart in accord with Christian faith and moral conversion to the political cause of emancipation.

Her novel's graphic portrayal of flogging, murder, suicide, infanticide, and sexual assault all serve to demonstrate how "the peculiar institution" brutalized human beings, degrading both whites and blacks. Yet Stowe recognized that her readers might be most deeply moved by witnessing slavery's abhorrent destruction of families. She saw the nation's union—if not its very soul—threatened by disuniting horror of a

11. Ibid., 56, 101.

system that could legally put asunder wives from husbands and remove children from their mothers. An emotionally charged episode early in the story shows Eliza Harris, child in arms, desperately fleeing across ice floes in the Ohio River to save her child, Harry, from bondage and forced separation.

Harriet Beecher Stowe's preoccupation in *Uncle Tom's Cabin* with the destruction of familial bonds owed much to her personal experience of bereavement. Though she eventually gave birth to seven children, she was traumatized by the loss in 1849 of her infant son, Charley, during a cholera epidemic that swept through Cincinnati. Sunk for a time in despair, she nonetheless found by 1851, when she felt divinely prompted to begin writing *Uncle Tom's Cabin*, that her maternal grief and indignation were undergoing a creative transformation. Still anguished by Charley's death, she felt her private pain transfigured into broader compassion for the plight of slave mothers, and she felt a new, evangelical passion to stir the hearts of fellow Americans through her writing.

To be sure, several circumstances moved Stowe to action. Passage of the Fugitive Slave Law in 1850 was one such provocation. Another was the vision she reported receiving, during a communion service at First Parish Church in Brunswick, Maine, of a slave—the prototype of her character Tom—brutally beaten to death. However, a pivotal reason to write this book with her "heart's blood" was the opportunity she felt to transform her private anguish into a public plea for conversion, to find gain for others in her experience of maternal loss. As Stowe explained in a letter she wrote in 1853,

> I can only see that when a Higher Being has purposes to be accomplished, he can make even "a grain of mustard seed" the means—
>
> I wrote what I did because as a woman, as a mother I was oppressed & broken-hearted, with the sorrows & injustice I saw, because as a Christian I felt the dishonor to Christianity—because as a lover of my country I trembled at the coming day of wrath.—
>
> It is no merit in the sorrowful that they weep, or to the oppressed & smothering that they gasp & struggle, nor to me, that I *must* speak for the oppressed—who cannot speak for themselves.[12]

---

12. Cited in Hedrick, *Harriet Beecher Stowe*, 237.

Stowe's enormously influential book spoke indeed for the oppressed, while dramatizing its author's confidence in the saving, transformative force of love. For Stowe, such love was reflected particularly in the divine beauty of maternal care and in the self-sacrificing generosity of a character like Tom. Modeled in part on an escaped slave, Tom betrays only a few minor traits that accord with his disrepute in today's common parlance as an "Uncle Tom." So it is a mistake to interpret Tom's self-abnegation and nonviolent resistance as a form of docility demeaning to African Americans. For example, many readers or would-be readers of Stowe's book forget that Tom, in his generous yet boldly assertive love, defies the slaveholding tyrant Simon Legree more than once. When Legree orders Tom to flog a fellow slave, he flatly refuses, to the amazement of all who witness his response: "'Mas'r,'" he says calmly, "'I *never* shall do it, —*never*.'"[13] On another occasion, Tom stands up to Legree so firmly that he reduces this infamous character to blubbering desperation. Tom demonstrates that he will die rather than disclose the whereabouts of two fugitive slaves named Cassy and Emmeline, a refusal to cooperate that enables them to escape Legree's clutches. What Legree wants most is not Tom's destruction but information—which Tom possesses—concerning these fugitives. But though Legree wields the immense force given him by law, custom, and the whip, Tom defeats this purpose, rendering him powerless:

> "Well, Tom!" said Legree, walking up, and seizing him grimly by the collar of his coat, and speaking through his teeth, in a paroxysm of determined rage,
>
> "Do you know I've made up my mind to KILL you?"
>
> "It's very likely, Mas'r," said Tom calmly.
>
> "I *have*," said Legree, with a grim terrible calmness, "*done—just— that—thing*, Tom, unless you'll tell me what you know about these yer gals!"
>
> Tom stood silent.
>
> "D'ye hear?" said Legree, stamping, with a roar like that of an incensed lion. "Speak!"
>
> "*I han't got nothing to tell, Mas'r.*" said Tom with a slow, firm, deliberate utterance."
>
> "Speak!" thundered Legree, striking him furiously.
>
> "Do you know anything?"
>
> "I know, Mas'r; but I can't tell anything. I *can die.*"[14]

13. Stowe, *Uncle Tom's Cabin*, 507.

14. Ibid., 582.

What Stowe sets forth here, in the person of Tom, is a transformational ideal of spirituality that involves not simply a redistribution but a
more radical redefinition of power. Thus Legree, once he encounters the
full force of Tom's spirit-centered strength, "could not hide from himself
that his power over his bond thrall was somehow gone."[15] Just as Stowe
welcomed the process by which she was able to refashion her own grief
and despair into powerful testimony on behalf of "those who cannot speak
for themselves," so also she dramatizes in *Uncle Tom's Cabin* the prospect
of embracing a Transfiguration of worldly power—a regenerative hope
equivalent to participation in the transcendent Kingdom of God.

By way of exposing one further view of how a Transfiguration
gospel can refashion conceptions of the social order we inhabit, the
career and writings of William Porcher DuBose are worth considering. Commonly described as the most original theologian of the U.S.
Episcopal Church, DuBose lived through the tumultuous era of the War
Between the States—as did Harriet Beecher Stowe. And like Stowe, he
was much engaged in the social anxieties preceding and following that
momentous struggle, wherein he served as both officer and chaplain. Yet
Stowe, raised in New England within a celebrated family whose members included several social reformers, was a confirmed abolitionist.
DuBose, in contrast, was a lifelong Southerner from South Carolina. He
was raised in a slaveholding environment, countenanced slavery prior to
the war, and fought for the Confederacy.

DuBose's perception that his side would lose the war figured, in
fact, among the "turning points" of the spiritual journey that he would
later describe in a personal narrative published in 1912 toward the close
of his life. He recalls that one lonely night in wartime, following an episode in which his brigade had been routed, he felt a premonition of final
defeat come upon him. At that moment it seemed as though "the end
of the world" was coming upon him, as decisively as when the ancient
Romans faced the close of their era. Despite the shock and pain of all
this, he was drawn that evening to redevote "myself wholly and only to
God, and to the work and life of His Kingdom, whatever and wherever
that might be."[16]

The transformation of loss thus became subsumed into his devel-
oping theological vision, as did a post-war chastening of his attitudes

15. Ibid., 558.
16. DuBose, *Turning Points*, 49–50.

toward slavery and a commitment to reconciling the doctrinal truths of classic Christianity with those uncovered by the "new science" of his day. Within the several books DuBose produced after the war, while serving as professor at the University of the South in Sewanee, Tennessee, his bid to incorporate the altered worldview suggested by organic evolution into his own version of process theology may be his most noteworthy and enduring contribution to intellectual understanding. Central to his outlook was the idea that Christ's incarnation should be seen as an all-encompassing process of dynamic metamorphosis. This process touches everything, since DuBose affirmed with Saint Paul in 2 Corinthians 5:17 that in Christ "all things . . . have become new,"[17] including the transformation of humanity. A sermon he preached in 1911, on the feast of the Transfiguration, aptly sounds this theme in harmony with the forty-year store of recollections he had by then accumulated at Sewanee. (The sermon has been reprinted as the Appendix to this book.)

DuBose offered the sermon during a commemorative reunion with former students held in his honor at Sewanee, following almost four decades of active association with the University of the South as professor, chaplain, and dean. It seems that this community had recently faced some disheartening fears and difficulties. DuBose addresses that challenge by asking, "How can we acquire the secret of making the old ever new, and keeping it so?" Reflecting on the larger course of his career, he begins by confiding to his listeners, "On this one occasion of my life, in this place, and upon this spot, I may presume to be somewhat personal." As the University of the South stands on a plateau, DuBose found it natural to link the mountain setting of the biblical Transfiguration with this local topography. He concludes, in fact, with a poignant reminder: "We stand today together upon an exceeding high mountain—upon this mountain, not only as itself transfigured, but as itself no less a Mount of Transfiguration." Appropriately, too, he draws on kinetic spatial imagery in describing how the Incarnation involves both God's "oneness with us (coming down)—and on our part (going up) of faith, hope, and love that make us one with Him."

A central theme of DuBose's sermon is that "We do indeed live only in our supreme moments" and that the Transfiguration episode offers a crystallization of all such moments of truth. What most of us sense only in moments of peak experience was for Jesus a perpetually realized

17. Ibid., 117.

communion with the divine—though only briefly revealed as such to his disciples. So "how is it," DuBose asks, that "our Lord Himself could live so continuously and so high?" And what relevance does Jesus' glorification on the mount bear for the rest of us mortals?

DuBose emphasizes that this vision of Jesus' metamorphosis—though it signifies no actual change in his nature—dramatizes for us the high promise of human destiny. "For what," he asks," is Jesus Christ but God in us and we in God? Accordingly, "what is the Cross but the actual process by which all that is not God dies in us, and all that is lives and grows in us."[18] Yet DuBose understood this process—whether charted through individual lives, historical events, or the course of cosmic evolution—to be gradual, often invisible. In emphasizing the process character of God's incarnation and humanity's deification, DuBose was plainly influenced by the new science of his day. Having elsewhere claimed that "the general fact or truth of evolution . . . can scarcely now be questioned," he found it supporting his confidence in "the manifest interconnection and interrelation running through all life." Evolution did not threaten but rather confirmed his godly faith that "all life is one." His transformational theology thus presumes what he called "the encosmic relation of God to the world"[19] and takes seriously the implications of organic evolution—or of that process earlier science called the "transmutation" or "transformation" of species. DuBose observed that Jesus, too, "took all the old things as they were, and He made them all living and new." But again, that process by which all things become new is slow, unpredictable, and often painful or destructive. Only retrospectively, as when one calls to mind certain "supreme moments" of crisis or ecstasy, might larger patterns of development begin to appear. Though "God and heaven are everywhere and always here if we could but see them,"[20] it is rarely possible to do so except in those "spots of time," as Wordsworth called them, discovered at points of crisis or illumination.

Among these "turning points" that DuBose elsewhere identifies within his own life journey are crucial stages in his religious conversion, as well as near-death episodes recalled from his wartime experience. Having nearly killed or been killed during a chance encounter at night with a Federal soldier from Pennsylvania, he later enjoyed a friendly

18. Ibid., 123, 115–16, 117, 118.

19. DuBose, from *The Reason of Life*, cited in *A DuBose Reader*, 149, 151.

20. DuBose, *Turning Points*, 117.

rapprochement with his former foe. This Union veteran even came to meet him in Sewanee and reported that "some mysterious force had held his hand and prevented him" from shooting DuBose when they first met alone in wartime, as enemies, on another mountain.

Just as DuBose lived long enough to see this particular relationship metamorphose quite radically, so also he came to appreciate the process of transmutation by which his own political and social attitudes changed—partly as a consequence of suffering defeat in the war. By 1918, the year of his death, he had witnessed momentous changes in his region, nation, and global society through the close of World War I. Such alterations were often traumatic. And DuBose, having participated actively in several of these changes, underscored humanity's role as co-creator with God in the ongoing drama of Transfiguration.

In this respect the theology of William Porcher DuBose anticipates that of Desmond Tutu. Still, even in his later years, DuBose articulated views concerning slavery and African Americans that must today be regarded as less than fully enlightened. So the process of transformation remained for him—and, I dare say, for us—incomplete. Though limited in the topical reach of his social criticism, DuBose saw in the Transfiguration episode a compelling vision of future development presenting both hope for humanity and a challenge to be seized. "If it be true that we do live, if only in our supreme moments," he reasoned, "is not every moment in which we have so lived a new and sufficient proof to us of the eternal and infinite reality of the Life Indeed?—and a new and compelling incentive to us to live it, though it take us forever, and we have to pass through deaths and resurrections, to do so."[21]

21. Ibid., 120.

9

Another Metamorphosis: The Greening of Religious Culture

CHARGED AS IT IS with poetic and visionary meaning, the gospel episode of the Transfiguration resists literal-minded interpretations. No wonder it is sometimes regarded, even by church leaders, as embarrassing or unimportant. Writer Madeleine l'Engle reports her disappointment at finding one year that no church in her neighborhood saw fit to celebrate the Feast Day of August 6. "You'd think," she muses, "that in the church year we would celebrate it with as much excitement and joy as we do Christmas and Easter." But while "We give it lip service when we talk about "mountain-top experiences," she laments that "mostly we ignore it, and my guess is that this is because we are afraid. . . . We are afraid of the Transfiguration for much the same reason that people are afraid that theatre is a 'lie,' that a story isn't 'true,' that art is somehow immoral, carnal and not spiritual."[1]

If anything, though, the Transfiguration warrants renewed attention today because its expansive implications address present-day concerns with a symbolic potential that is all too rare in our postindustrial culture. I am thinking here particularly about ecological ramifications of the metamorphosis story. To be sure, environmental rhetoric, including frequent commendations of "sustainability," has—in principle, if not always in practice—gained popular favor in recent years. So, too, has the idea of "greening" statements of faith that have otherwise, in Western religious tradition, focused rather narrowly on human welfare and the quest for personal salvation. Theoretically, at least, earth-friendly religion is in vogue. Today there is no lack of theologically informed, published commentary available to those wishing to discover, at least

1. L'Engle, *Walking on Water*, 80.

in intellectual terms, how the ideals of Christian faith converge with a commitment to ecological restoration.

Nonetheless, symbols and rituals through which someone of our culture might actually apprehend that relation—spiritually, emotionally, and liturgically, as well as theologically—remain in short supply. For that matter, the denatured, mass-produced climate of today's commercial society affords less exposure to elemental, integrative symbolism of any sort than would be available in societies that retain a conscious connection with the agricultural foundations of life. Although one may fairly suppose that the Easter Vigil's symbolic vocabulary of water, fire, word, and light remains comprehensible to those modern worshippers who encounter such liturgy, it is harder to gain inward access to that larger figurative realm that the New Testament evokes with reference to sheep and goats, wheat harvests, olive trees, and mustard seeds. Yet we cannot live, or at least cannot live abundantly, without the imaginative and spiritual sustenance of symbols. And symbols cannot be constructed at will by artisans or planning groups. Rooted in sensible objects from the material world, they are capable of engaging the human psyche in planes of reality not only seen but unseen, metaphysical as well as emotive and intellective, subconscious as well as conscious.

So what figures or icons might qualify as the chief symbolic representations of present-day environmental consciousness? And which of these, if any, seem to be charged with religious significance? The most frequently referenced figure of ecology's "one earth" outlook, emphasizing the beauty yet rare fragility of our home planet, must be the 1972 full earth photo taken by Apollo 17 astronauts while headed toward the moon. Since the nineteenth century, the U.S. environmental movement has also, at various times, attributed broader representational value to certain endangered and threatened animals, plants, or places and has taken steps to protect them. John Muir's 1920 article titled "Save the Redwoods" highlighted the vulnerability of one such vegetative organism, just as Muir's rhapsodic accounts of Yosemite have contributed to memorializing that locale as an epitome of the American sublime. Other national sites that have gained symbolic status would include Walden Pond, by virtue of Thoreau's classic book, the Grand Canyon, and Arches National Monument in Utah, as celebrated by Ed Abbey. And as a token of environmental degradation, mention of Love Canal in Niagara, New York, calls to mind the perils of toxic waste, just as the

Gulf Coast oil spill of 2010 has already come to symbolize the reckless endangerment to ecosystems posed by untested technology and profit-hungry multinationals.

Animal species that have won symbolic recognition in ecological terms often display traits or shapes that humans find attractive. Thus, Rachel Carson underscored the threat to birds—including robins, doves, wrens, and other species not typically viewed as endangered—in the landmark discourse of her *Silent Spring*. With the benefit of Gary Snyder's poem titled "Mother Earth: Her Whales," several species of these intelligent yet threatened marine mammals became signature animals for conservationists toward the close of the twentieth century. Imperatives to preserve endangered wolves and polar bears have lately attracted similar attention.

None of these conservationist icons carries any particular linkage to a religious tradition, however. While biblically grounded *themes* of stewardship, the land's sabbath, and creation are commonly invoked by Christian environmentalists, comparable *symbols* of ecological integrity have rarely gained much favor or attention. The figure of the earth as a well-tended garden probably comes closest to such a representation. In literalistic terms, the Garden of Eden portrayed in the Book of Genesis may seem remote from circumstances of life that urban dwellers today recognize as comparable to their own. Yet this primal green space of the Garden remains potentially relevant insofar as its image of ecological community embodies the religious principle of shalom, thus displaying an integrative harmony between humans and the rest of earthly Creation. Ecologically, this shalom principle carries acknowledgment of a divine rather than human sovereignty over the planet. To gain a comprehensive view of nature as God's creation, we need to supplement endorsement of the calmer Edenic model with recognition of that wilder world of untamed creatures—including the lion, hawk, mountain goat, and crocodile—poetically described in the Book of Job.[2] Nonetheless, the Garden of Eden expresses the ideal of cultivating a cooperative rather than a totally controlling relation to the nonhuman world.[3]

---

2. See also the discerning exegetical commentaries on this point offered by Gordis, "Job and Ecology," 189–201; and by McKibben, *The Comforting Whirlwind*.

3. For a detailed exploration of how this biblical garden image can be related to real-world ecosystems and economic issues, see Gottfried, *Economics, Ecology*.

From time to time, some have aspired to invent or discover new religious symbols associated with ecological restoration. A few modern writers have succeeded in formulating ecological fables that carry mythical and spiritual resonance. One such tale, presented in the guise of a personal reminiscence, is Loren Eiseley's "The Star Thrower."[4] A less familiar story, associated with the self-sacrifice of Pascagoula Indians and the sacred spirit of a watercourse, is recounted by Mark I. Wallace as an overture to Wallace's provocative exposition of ecotheology.[5] It is rarely possible, though, to manufacture organically evocative symbols. They must be reconceived either directly from nature or from some venerable course of shared cultural experience, scriptural or otherwise. As Ralph Waldo Emerson observed, the most potent symbols and symbolic language derive from "nature the symbol," from that creative flux and energy constituting "the life of the Universe."[6]

And yet, because current environmental perils pose a moral and spiritual crisis for our culture, the need to embrace a compelling symbology of earth-restoration has never been more acute. Moreover, as Bishop Kallistos Ware points out, the figurative revelation of a transfigured world is uniquely suited to address both the symbolic impoverishment and the ecological crisis of our age. Bishop Ware goes so far as to declare that "Within the Gospel story the Transfiguration of Christ stands out as the ecological event par excellence."[7]

On what grounds, though, might one regard the Transfiguration as Christianity's defining ecological symbol for our time? Its representation of re-creative divine energy is, for one thing, dynamic rather than static. It reveals that which Emerson, perceived, albeit in non-Christian terms, as an elemental "flowing or metamorphosis" at the heart of nature.[8] The import of the Transfiguration is effectively mystical, rather than purely didactic or moralistic. And it is genuinely radical, in the sense of reaching to the very roots of our relation to matter, energy, and ultimate reality. More elemental than the now-familiar church custom of blessing pets and other animals in honor of Saint Francis, an appealing but limited ges-

---

4. I comment further on the character of this work in *Making Nature Sacred*, 172–3.

5. Wallace, *Finding God*, 1–6.

6. Emerson, "The Poet," 228, 233.

7. Ware, "Safeguarding the Creation," 89.

8. Emerson, *Selections*, 230.

ture of ecological care beyond the species boundary, the Transfiguration sounds the life-changing depths of Christian spirituality.

For me, as for Bishop Ware, the visual representation that most richly reveals the gospel's inner sense of a metamorphosed new creation is the apse mosaic found in the Basilica of Saint Apollinaris in Classe, near Ravenna, Italy (see fig. 4). Like Saint Augustine's famed apostrophe to God as beauty personified in the *Confessions*, it is an image that confronts us simultaneously as "so ancient and so new." Ancient, to begin with, in a literal sense since its sixth-century visualization of the Transfiguration is among the earliest extant. Ancient because it invokes elemental landscape features of rock, mountain, vegetation, and light. Ancient because its imagery recalls not only themes drawn from Hebraic and Christian scriptures, but also a pastoral ideal commonly evoked in pagan, Greco-Roman culture. This mosaic of the Byzantine school looks decidedly premodern, too, by virtue of the flattened, non-perspectival style in which its figures are rendered.

Figure 4

How, then, can this ancient mosaic also seem new? I remember marveling, when I had a chance to gaze at this extraordinary production during a visit to Ravenna some years ago, that a work so venerable could retain such freshness and vivid color. A work of such startling originality could, it seems, have been completed just yesterday. And while this patristic-era mosaic dates from early in the church's history, it illustrates a novel way of rendering the Transfiguration that remains sui generis. Unlike other ancient renderings, the particular artistry represented here initiated no school of imitation. It is remarkable, in fact, that such an intricately developed, theologically interpretive work of this kind, as opposed to a more straightforward visualization of the gospel episode, appeared as early as it did.

Instead of trying to picture the synoptic narrative directly, to show Jesus glorified on a lonely site atop a prominence in Galilee beside his disciples and the two prophets, the Ravenna mosaic embodies Jesus' presence more subtly within a vision that encompasses human society and the church universal, as well as the local faith community and the whole order of natural creation. This last recognition of a blessed and potentially transfigured creation is conveyed by setting both biblical and nonbiblical personages together on the common ground of a lush green tapestry. Within the larger scene, Moses, Elijah, Christ, Saint Apollinaris, and the three favored apostles are linked not only to the other apostles, but to the whole company of the faithful in subsequent ages. The picture's expanse of meadow signifies, among other things, that beauty and harmony suffusing God's garden world in the original creation. At the same time, it reflects the transformed, eschatological vision of paradise wrought by Christ in the new creation.[9] Moreover, it images details—including pinewoods, palm trees, shrubs, and birds—that link the mosaic's symbolic landscape to features of the actual Mediterranean landscape found in the basilica's immediate region.

It may seem odd at first that the human figure outlined most prominently within this tableau is not Christ but Saint Apollinaris, presumptive martyr and first bishop of Ravenna. Yet in the light of Transfiguration, this displacement becomes altogether fitting. It is particularly germane to life in the aftermath of Christ's Ascension. For the unknown artist portrays in this mosaic not the historical Jesus of Nazareth, but a cosmic Christ whose diffused and transformative presence fills all things—and most visibly sustains the local faith community of God's saints. As *alter Christus*, then, Saint Apollinaris assumes here the role of Episcopal suc-

9. Andreopoulos, *Metamorphosis*, 119–20. In addition to the commentaries by Andreopoulos and Ware, useful remarks about the artistry of these apse mosaics are provided by Nes in *The Uncreated Light*, 12–23 and 74–84.

cessor on earth of Christ, the Good Shepherd. Apollinaris fulfills this pastoral office, clothed in a white dalmatic and purple chasuble embroidered with bees, this last detail testifying to his eloquence. He is shown to stand, hands outstretched in the priestly *orans* posture, directly above an altar where the sacrament of Eucharistic transformation would continue to be celebrated throughout the ages. In effect, then, an imagistic representation of Apollinaris continues to preside sacerdotally over a sacred space not only dedicated to him, but where his bodily remains were said at one time to have been placed, thereby establishing him as one with Christ on this site in a decidedly physical mode of "real presence."

Because Apollinaris appears here as shepherd, it follows that the faithful should, in accord with biblical precedent throughout both testaments, be portrayed as a flock of sheep. Yet the sense of them conveyed through this charming figure is scarcely that of dullness and docility. Sheltered amid the beauty of lilies, roses, and fertile meadow, these sheep display instead an alert and upright dignity, of the sort attributable to that speaker in lamb's clothing so familiar in the twenty-third Psalm. The symbology of Christ as Lamb of God probably informs this picture as well. For that matter, whether or not by conscious intention of its artistic creator, the scene's representation of humans in animal form ends up visually undercutting the idea of a strict dichotomy between *anthropos* and animal orders of being. That humans share something of divine life with other animals, that shifts or metamorphoses in one's life form can occur across evolutionary registers of animate life—all of this, of course, underlies Asian religious views of reincarnation. Native American mythologies, too, frequently dramatize through shape-shifting tales the porousness of boundaries between human and animal identity, to underscore earth's common sustenance of all. The Lakota shaman Black Elk, for example, evidences such views through the creation story he tells of a beautiful woman's disappearance into the shape of a white, sacred bison.[10]

While admitting some vertical distinction between earthly and heavenly realms, the Saint Apollinaris mosaic illustrates more forcefully the essential unity of the cosmos. In this scene's *omnium gatherum*, we find clefted rocks, trees, flowers, shrubs, birds, sheep, and divine Being enclosed within the same space as human beings from disparate periods of history. Humanity is thus aligned or identified here not only with ani-

10. Black Elk, *Black Elk Speaks*, 2–4.

mals but with plant life and inanimate creatures as well. And by virtue of the incarnation, humans such as Apollinaris are shown to be allied not only with nonhumans, but also with the divine. So in present-day terms, this continuity of creation reflects a comprehensively ecological vision that embraces yet surpasses the material world.

The mosaic's sacred geometry is worth pondering, too. Notice how the oval shape of the apse curvature encloses a celestial sphere in figure 4 and, in turn, the contrasting rectilinear outline of a cross. Although the Transfiguration's mountain setting is not pictured directly, the overall design nonetheless conveys some sense of scaled being and ascent, especially through the pattern of a broad-based yet narrowing ellipsis. Within this oversized mandorla, a counterpart of the halo attached to Saint Apollinaris appears in the larger sphere above his head, a zone that conjoins heaven and earth—and whose circularity expresses the perfection and endlessness of God. Both the astronomical heights of creation and the mystery of uncreated light are contained herein.

The starry blue coloring within this celestial sphere seems to represent the highest cosmological reaches of creation, in contrast with the prevailing brown and green earth tones below. In light of the creation described at the start of Genesis, the blue shading painted across the basilica's vaulting images not only the skies, but also the elemental waters above and below the great vault of heaven. All in all, the Transfiguration's cosmic meaning could scarcely be illustrated more effectively.

Centered amid the stars, though, is a cross (see fig. 5). In its geometric form, the figure simply draws to awareness a grid of elemental reality—by signaling the four cardinal directions and by marking a point of intersection between earth and heaven, human and divine, time and eternity. But this shape also draws us firmly back to earth. It marks a harder reality than the green meadows. As the cross of Christ, it dramatizes above all the inescapable yet redeeming reality of affliction—and of God's willingness to suffer *in* and *with* the whole creation. Bishop Ware points out that "between the two hills Tabor and Calvary there is no great distance," since "if we divorce Christ's Transfiguration from his Crucifixion, then we distort the meaning of both."[11]

---

11. Ware, "Safeguarding the Creation," 91.

Figure 5

That Jesus' Transfiguration takes place within the shadow of the cross, that metamorphosis requires an encounter with affliction—these by-now familiar themes, played out through centuries of theological tradition, already find clear visual expression in this mosaic. It is striking that only the face of Jesus—not his body—should be inscribed, in miniature, upon the cross. Such diminishment is fitting, however, since the post-resurrection, transfigured body of Christ now extends, in effect, throughout the Church and illumines the whole of creation. The mosaic's captivating image of a human face amid the stars reminds me of how Dante's narrator in *Paradiso*, beholding at last the radiant source of that Love "that moves the sun and the other stars,"[12] is amazed to

12. Alighieri, *Paradiso*, 485.

discover a human likeness at the divine apex of his ascent through the empyrean.

Yet while the sign of the cross surely marks this visualization of the Transfiguration, the cross has itself undergone here a metamorphosis—from instrument of torture to emblem of beauty and triumph. In the mosaic, spangled in gold against a heavenly blue, it appears indeed as a thing of beauty. And insofar as beauty mirrors, theologically, the harmony and blessed ecology by which the interdependence of all things is played out in the dance of God and creation, we can appreciate why the Transfiguration has so often been called a feast of beauty. In one ancient apocryphal text, for example, the Ethiopic *Apocalypse of Peter*, Moses and Elijah appear on the holy mountain with a beauty "that no mouth is able to utter," because their "aspect was astonishing and wonderful." Jesus, meanwhile, shines "above crystal"; and "like the flower of roses is . . . the color of his aspect. . . . And upon his shoulders and on their foreheads was a crown of nard woven of fair flowers. As the rainbow in the water, so was their hair." This anonymous author goes on to describe Jesus' opening, on the occasion of the Transfiguration, fresh awareness of earth's loveliness as well: "And he showed us a great garden, open, full of fair trees and blessed fruits, and of the odor of perfumes. The fragrance thereof was pleasant and came even to us. And thereof saw I much fruit."[13]

Part of the mosaic's beauty derives from its boldly affectionate embrace of disparate elements upon a common space. Plants, mineral earth and soil, stars, and wild birds blend happily here with domestic animals, heavenly beings, and humans—all pictured as belonging to the grand ecology of God's *oikos*, or household.

As the mosaic demonstrates, the Transfiguration qualifies as a feast of beauty as well as a festival of creation—and of new creation. In the gospel accounts of Mark and Matthew, the metamorphosis episode took place "after six days," traditionally interpreted by the Church Fathers as a symbolic reference to the days of creation. As Rowan Williams observes, "In the Gospels, the transfiguration story is introduced with the apparently innocent words, 'after six days' (in Matthew and Mark), or 'after about eight days' (in Luke). From early times, commentators have said that this is an allusion to the days of creation: the transfiguration is the climax of the creative work of God, either the entrance into the joy and

---

13. Cited in Andreopoulos, *Metamorphosis*, 39–40.

repose of the seventh day or the beginning of the new creation, depending on what kind of symbolism you want to use."[14] To revere the beauty of creation, as the basilica's mosaic so manifestly does, is to recover a motive for earthcare that is at the heart of present-day ecotheology. Such love for the earth and appreciation of godliness in the material world must be, as Teilhard de Chardin often insisted, the hallmark of Christian piety in a post-Darwinian era. Epitomized by the Transfiguration, a vision of nature as wondrous Creation is also more likely to inspire environmental responsibility than a purely moralistic, guilt-driven form of religious teaching.

Reflecting further on the ecotheology of Transfiguration, as suggested by discrete features of the mosaic's landscape imagery, I am particularly drawn to consider the trees represented there. Though the gospel accounts of Jesus' metamorphosis make no mention of trees, arboreal life has long held a special place in reflections and writing about the natural world. Consider, for example, the many tales of humanity's primordial connection to a world tree or to rites conducted in sacred groves that have flourished for millennia in diverse cultures. Landmark trees, sometimes shadowed by recollection of archaic and Canaanite practices, abound in both Old and New Testaments. They range from the oaks of Mamre where Abraham encounters three numinous visitors, through images of a towering cedar of Lebanon, along with noteworthy arboreal allusions throughout the gospels and Saint Paul's epistles, to the Book of Revelation's vision of a great tree in the New Jerusalem, bearing twelve kinds of fruit and leaves "for the healing of the nations." Within the overall biblical narrative, a major line of symbolic association can be traced from the tree of life in Genesis to the wood of Jesus' cross—later interpreted, as in the sixth-century century hymn of Fortunatus, as a tree of glory and transformative regrowth of the tree of life.

What is it about trees that so perennially stirs the imagination, wins our sympathy, and speaks to the soul? In the case of redwoods, great oaks, or the banyan tree, part of the fascination seems to derive simply from our awareness that life forms of appreciable size—whose life spans far surpass our own—live in our midst. It is marvelous to think that some individual trees that were alive when Jesus walked the earth continue to endure.

14. Williams, *The Dwelling of the Light*, 8; see also Andreopoulos, 45, 147.

Then too, trees connect disparate realms of space as well as time. Rooted in chthonic depths of an underworld beneath our normal sight, they nonetheless share a place with us on earth's surface while reaching well above us into the heavens. No wonder they have so often been regarded as friends to meditation, channels of access to transcendent wisdom and experience. It seems altogether fitting that Gautama, the Buddha, should have been described as attaining enlightenment beneath a pipal or bodhi tree (*Ficus religiosa*), a species that even before his birth had gained recognition in India as sacred.[15] J. R. R. Tolkien, who in his *Lord of the Rings* trilogy dramatized the unsettling and otherworldly quality we sometimes feel in the midst of dense forest, also wrote a short story, "Leaf by Niggle." Apparently inspired by the destruction of a "great-limbed poplar," Tolkien describes the transformation of his main character in the light of Christian spirituality and in relation to a Great Tree.[16] Trees testify to something beyond our own stature, to a life larger than ours.

At the same time, there can be something comforting and quite familiar about the presence of trees. Trees lend beauty and grace to an otherwise barren landscape. And they often help to frame or define our human sense of place, as poems such as Robert Frost's "Tree at My Window" so poignantly demonstrate. I can still recall from childhood seeing the anguish with which my father, who was not a demonstrative person, reacted to the demise of an aged elm tree that had adorned the back yard of our home in upstate New York. "Like losing an old friend," he sighed. So it is oddly appropriate that intensely conservation-minded folks should sometimes be called "tree-huggers," albeit in scorn. Henry Thoreau wrote unashamedly of sensing amid a gentle rain that nearby pine needles "expanded and swelled with sympathy and befriended me" and of the affection that led him to pay "many a visit to particular trees"[17] in the course of his daily sauntering in the neighborhood of Concord, Massachusetts.

As sources of fruits, nuts, paper, wood products, shade, and oxygen, trees provide many practical benefits to humans beyond their induce-

---

15. Altman, *Sacred Trees*, 39, 163.

16. See Tolkien's remarks on the inspiration for his tale in the Introductory Note to "Tree and Leaf," 2; I offer an interpretation of the story in question in "The Interior Progress," 2–15.

17. Thoreau, *Walden*, 120, 181.

ment to meditation. Though trees appear to stand still, science confirms them to be sites of dynamic transformation. Photosynthesis, oxygen and carbon dioxide exchanges, hydrological cycles—we know that all of these processes and more take place within and around these ostensibly static organisms. Many of the poems in Wendell Berry's collection, aptly titled *A Timbered Choir*, testify not only to the author's long emotional association with trees, but also to their spiritual gifts or "benefaction"—and to the correspondingly paradoxical tension between stillness and motion that they embody. One such poem describes the process of reforestation by which "great trees" gradually appear in an undisturbed lot. The piece begins with language paced to evoke the measured growth it describes: "Slowly, slowly they return / To the small woodland let alone." Instead of observing these growths as a detached onlooker, though, the speaker internalizes the mystery of their silence, their apparently still yet dynamic life. The poet, seeking Sabbath rest, aspires to emulate the absolute calm with which they "stand in waiting all around / Uprisings of their native ground." Berry imagines these creatures not merely entering upon but indeed hallowing this place made native both for them and for him:

> Patient as stars, they build in air
> Tier after tier a timbered choir,
> Stout beams upholding weightless grace
> Of song, a blessing on this place.[18]

Unlike the silent and "bare ruin'd choirs" of Shakespeare's famous sonnet,[19] the expansive limbs of this "timbered choir" do support birdsong while tracing spacious designs in air. Great trees, despite their seemingly inert solidity, support vital processes involving light and energy, microorganisms, motile fluids, and the exchange of atmospheric gasses.

As envisioned in Berry's poem, the dynamic of this physical synergism corresponds to a divine economy of grace and transformation:

> Receiving sun and giving shade,
> Their life's a benefaction made,
> And is a benediction said
> Over the living and the dead.[20]

18. Berry, "Slowly, slowly they return," *A Timbered Choir*, 83.

19. Shakespeare, Sonnet 73.

20. Berry, "Slowly, slowly they return," *A Timbered Choir*, 83.

For Berry, the seasonal lapse of foliage, reflecting yet another cycle of metamorphosis, qualifies as a fortunate fall. The energy captured in the trees' "brightened leaves" enables humans "To walk on radiance, amazed" and inspires the poet's closing benediction: "Oh light come down to earth, be praised." Thus, the multilayered metamorphosis enacted through and within these "great trees" parallels the transformation of human awareness described through the course of Berry's poem.

Mount Tabor, traditionally identified with the mount of Transfiguration, has been admired for profuse vegetation that includes flowering almond trees. Mountain-clinging trees and shrubs appear in several of the relevant icon paintings. It is fitting, then, that trees—in scriptural texts as well as literature of the Christian era—so commonly convey the sense of a divine presence in creation. In the imaginative light of Transfiguration, ordinary trees look less like inert fixtures than like living icons reflecting something of divine energy and life. Literary artists have thus found in the arboreal growth pattern of leaf, branch, and root an emblem of life itself. So a meditative gaze at or through some particular tree can epitomize discovery of Creation's transparency, its underlying spirit and metamorphic process.

This point is memorably illustrated in Annie Dillard's contemporary prose classic, *Pilgrim at Tinker Creek* (1974). Throughout this extended essay, the author endeavors to describe the world in the light of transfigured seeing. From her chosen window on the world near Virginia's Blue Ridge, she looks at many common creatures—including muskrats, fish, domestic animals, birds, and all manner of insects. But more than once, her gaze fastens on trees.

In a chapter aptly entitled "Seeing," Dillard recounts cases in which people blind from birth received immediate sight through the intervention of medical science. One young girl, newly sighted, was apparently so struck at seeing for the first time what a tree really looked like that she announced she saw lights in it. Strongly impressed by reading of the episode and alert to its iconic import, Dillard waited to receive a comparable rediscovery of the luminosity and energy hidden at the heart of things. Such perception would be the latter-day counterpart of transfigurative seeing, granted if at all through grace and after long interior training. Dillard writes that one day she, too, witnessed the metamorphosis of an ordinary cedar into a tree of life:

> When her doctor took her bandages off and led her into the gar-
> den, the girl who was no longer blind saw "the tree with the lights
> in it." It was for this tree I searched through the peach orchards
> of summer, in the forests of fall and down winter and spring for
> years. Then one day I was walking along Tinker Creek thinking
> of nothing at all and I saw the tree with the lights in it. I saw
> the backyard cedar where the mourning doves roost charged and
> transfigured, each cell buzzing with flame. I stood on the grass
> with the lights in it, grass that was wholly fire, utterly focused and
> utterly dreamed. It was less like seeing than like being seen for
> the first time seen, knocked breathless by a powerful glance. The
> flood of fire abated, but I'm still spending the power.[21]

To envision each cell of the cedar buzzing with flame is, in effect, to
look beneath surfaces toward the creature's hidden life. It is to witness,
in the light of modern science, the interfusion of matter and energy. For
a moment, at least, Dillard can *see through* to nature's ultimate reality as
God's wondrously animated, multilayered creation. Hence for the author,
this episode illuminates the very process of metamorphosis, revealing to
her—and to us—the gracious transfiguration of ordinary things. Later in
the book she declares that "on that cedar tree shone, however briefly, the
steady inward flames of eternity."[22]

This illumination does not permanently dispel the darkness—life's
pain, waste, cruelty, and strife—whose enormity almost overwhelms
Dillard in *Pilgrim* and in *For the Time Being* (1999), her later sequence
of quizzical meditations. "Everywhere," she observes, "darkness and the
presence of the unseen appalls."[23] When the radiance fades, she leaves
us wondering whether divine darkness or simply a void surrounds the
flame-lit cedar.

Yet the beauty of the Transfiguration gospel also resides here—in
the enduring tension it sustains between glory and affliction, between
God's endtime and now. Like every great work of art, the mystery of
Christ's Transfiguration at once exhibits and transcends the immediacy
of our human experience. Thus, the Transfiguration remains a compelling icon of hope for personal, social, and cosmic transformation that
literature, too, can at least express if not effect.

21. Dillard, *Pilgrim*, 36.
22. Ibid., 81.
23. Ibid., 21.

But let us look again at those trees and shrubs portrayed in the apse mosaic of Saint Apollinaris. The palm trees, especially, recall not only the gospel descriptions of Jesus' entry into Jerusalem, but also the Jewish Feast of Tabernacles or Booths (Sukkot), which may be linked in turn to Peter's proposal to make three booths or tents on the mountain to honor Jesus, Moses, and Elijah. Branches of palm (*lulav*) were specified, in fact (Lev 23:40), as one of the materials to be used in constructing the makeshift shelters where Israelites lived during the joyous, seven-day Feast of Tabernacles.[24] Palm branches and palm trees also symbolized Jewish messianic expectations about history's fulfillment in the endtime,[25] so they extend appropriately across both the earthly and heavenly vertical zones of the mosaic. Originally a harvest festival, Tabernacles reminded Israelites of that austere, yet faith-centered period their ancestors had spent wandering in the desert. As a retreat from conditions of more settled ease, it amounted to something of a camping episode cum pilgrimage, as is still the case for some practicing Jews. It thus involved participants in a "back to nature" experience that for a time made them forest dwellers again—relatively exposed to the elements, with branches and leaves gathered closely around them. According to Nehemiah 8:15, the *sukkah,* or hut, could include branches of pines—also pictured in the mosaic together with palm trees and shrubs.

The end-of-summer feast of fecundity—centered on corn and grapes—from which Sukkot originated finds a counterpart in agriculturally linked Greek and Russian church customs for celebrating the Transfiguration. As part of these Eastern liturgies, the priest typically blesses natural signs of summer's end and of autumn's first fruits: grapes in Greek tradition and apples in Russian.[26] Celebrating the material order of creation, such practices honor the Transfiguration's cosmic meaning. So does the pictorial splendor of the basilica's apse mosaic.

24. See Andreopoulous, *Metamorphosis*, 56–60, 104–5, 120. Admittedly, though, questions have been raised about the extent to which and the manner in which the Transfiguration story should be linked to the Feast of Tabernacles: see Lee, *Transfiguration*, 19; and Heil, *The Transfiguration of Jesus*, 116–22.

25. On the plant symbolism represented here, see, in addition to Andreopoulous, Altman's *Sacred Trees*, 32, 120, 194. Tirosh-Samuelson confirms the point that the Sukkot festival offers "an example of the sanctification of nature in rabbinic Judaism" (28) in "Judaism and Ecology," 26–33.

26. Andreopoulous, *Metamorphosis*, 65–66.

The Trinitarian texture of the Transfiguration, and of Christian faith in general, can also be discerned in this mosaic. As in other iconographic representations, the Father's presence is signaled by the hand-of-God motif that appears toward top of the scene. The Logos, or Second Person of the Trinity, is made visible in the face and cross of Christ. It is not ordinarily possible to locate the Holy Spirit as a discrete presence in visual representations of the Transfiguration. The luminous cloud, commonly linked to the Spirit in verbal commentaries, simply does not figure in the icon tradition. But the scattered nimbus impressions, suggestive of cirrus clouds, that surround Moses, Elijah, and Christ in the celestial zone of the apse mosaic strike me as offering an exception to this rule. So the Spirit as Cloud and Light, set in close proximity to the Father's hand and the Son's cross, rounds out the tableau's cosmically comprehensive design.

But what difference does the Trinitarian perspective really make? What might it contribute to a Christian understanding of ecotheology and, in turn, to the metamorphosis of religious culture that deeper engagement with the Transfiguration promises to encourage?

As Jürgen Moltmann has explained, the doctrine of the Trinity should be seen as pivotal to a faith-centered vision of ecology, as well as to Christian faith more generally.[27] And that is so because of the light it casts on the nature of God and on how that nature relates to the whole of created nature. Perceptions that the Christian God of heaven stands distinctly *apart* from a spiritless order of nature and matter help to explain why, in today's cultural atmosphere, Abrahamic religions are rarely thought to supply a primary stimulus for loving nature and preserving the earth. For many, environmental passion seems more likely to be fueled by materialistic, Buddhist, or broadly pantheistic views of the natural world. Monotheism has lately been blamed for all sorts of ills, ranging from environmental degradation to tribal arrogance, intolerance, and complicity with violence. Admittedly, belief in a sort of monarchical monotheism,[28] combined with a misguided belief in humanity's right to exercise a purely self-serving "dominion" over God's earth, has figured historically in Christian faith and practice.

27. Moltmann, *God in Creation*, esp. 2, 15–16, 98, 212.

28. On the distinction between a "monarchical model" and an "organic model" of God's relation to the world, see Macquarrie, "Creation and Environment," 32–47.

Yet Trinitarian spirituality, as suggested in chapter 3, offers something quite distinctive by way of inspiring a latter-day "greening" of Christian faith. The scientific worldview of our time has led humanity toward an ever-deeper, detailed, and paradoxical appreciation of nature's marvels. In this cultural context, belief in an unqualified monotheism becomes increasingly problematic, since it threatens to disconnect Creator from Creation so thoroughly that the material world as a whole seems effectively spiritless, a kind of lifeless or ungodly commodity. No wonder neo-animist or pantheistic forms of "nature religion" have generally won more favor than orthodox Christianity among many of today's younger green-spirited souls.

Still, an unqualified pantheism raises serious difficulties as well. In view of contemporary scientific understanding, it becomes all the harder to suppose that a god resides "in" the trees in any simple, animistic sense or that God's unapproachable essence could be reduced to the transient motions of wind or molecule. Whether or not one regards nature as "fallen" in any theological sense, it seems evident that the non-human world—from a human point of view, at least—presents enough discontinuities, faults, and horrors to discourage outright worship. Even Emerson, in certain moods, admitted, "Nature, as we know her, is no saint."[29] C. S. Lewis argued that transcendent monotheism can actually heighten appreciation of nature's commonplace earthiness, as well as its potential for spiritual signification. For if nature is taken to be divine, pure and simple, it ceases to be sacramental. Lewis wrote, "It is surely because the natural objects are no longer taken to be themselves Divine that they can now be magnificent symbols of Divinity."[30]

By contrast, the mystery of the Holy Trinity honors the textured, elusive, and paradoxical character of cosmic reality. Sustaining the tension between material and immaterial apprehensions of life, it expresses the paradox of a Creator's transcendent yet radically immanent and incarnate relation to Creation. As Moltmann suggests, a Trinitarian conception of God as Father, Son, and Spirit envisions God's relation to the world not as a case of simple domination from a distance, but as a many-layered association, an infolding in community.[31]

This reference to community recalls the point that, for Trinitarian doctrine, an internal dynamic of community characterizes the godhead

29. Emerson, "Experience," 263.
30. Lewis, *Reflections*, 81–83.
31. Moltmann, *God in Creation*, 2.

itself, which constitutes both a unity and a community of persons, albeit not in the usual earthly sense. Theologically, then, the larger community of creation in which human beings live and move finds its center in a divine community of persons. And as Aldo Leopold observed, to develop an ecological ethic suited to our era requires our learning to conceive of nature not as a "commodity belonging to us" but as "a community to which we belong."[32] Hence the green logic for valuing belief in a Triune God. Participation in the interactive mystery of divine life points toward a model of earth ethics more profound than the "stewardship" ideal now favored in religious circles, which suffers the liability of suggesting a commodity-based rather than communitarian outlook. The gospels' and iconic representations of the Transfiguration suggest a divinely Trinitarian—and thus communitarian—apprehension of God and, by extension, of cosmic reality. The icons typically do this through a triadic blocking of persons and spatial zones.

The Holy Trinity presupposes not only a communitarian but also a dynamic understanding of divinity—and of divinity's relation to creation. Yet another ecological value of the Trinitarian vision, then, lies in its capacity to mediate, in a dynamic fashion, between the sacred otherness demanded by monotheism and the spiritual indwelling favored by pantheism or polytheism. Consistent with the Holy Spirit's ever-active, moving force across the face of creation, the Trinity affirms the presence of a force field of personalized energy *within* the Creator as well. Moltmann points out that "the trinitarian doctrine of creation suggests a pneumatological interpretation. The God who is present in the world and in every part of it, is the creative Spirit. It is not merely the spirit of God that is present in the evolving world; it is rather God the Spirit, with his uncreated and creative energies."[33]

What the disciples glimpse at the Transfiguration, and we through their eyes, is the luminescence of all these energies. The Transfiguration discloses that God's re-creative spirit continues, until the end of time, to inspire the redemptive metamorphosis of all things. Or, as Pierre Teilhard de Chardin, writing to his cousin, expressed the matter, "The

32. Leopold, *A Sand County Almanac*, xviii.

33. Moltmann, *God in Creation*, 212; see also Wallace's *Finding God*, which elaborates upon the notion of "the Holy Spirit as the fleshly, carnal bird God of the Bible who lives in all things and who enables in us a heartfelt desire to work toward the preservation of earth community in our time" (x).

Transfiguration has become a favorite feast of mine, because it expresses exactly what I love most in Our Lord and what I expect most ardently from him. May the blessed metamorphosis of the whole creation also take place within us, and before our eyes."[34]

Lines of development in modern science intersect in this regard with those in theology. Since the middle of the nineteenth century, secular learning in diverse spheres has continued to reinforce the impression that evolutionary change—developmental flux rather than changelessness— is the primary nature of nature. And in recent years the classic "balance of nature" paradigm, which saw ecosystems gaining stability as they approached climax, has been challenged by a newer "flux of nature" paradigm that emphasizes instead the inevitability of change and disturbance within ecosystems now perceived to be open.[35] It seems, nonetheless, that Christian culture has yet to assimilate Teilhard de Chardin's prophetic insight: that evolutionary theory cannot merely be accepted as compatible with revealed religion, but must be fully integrated with contemporary faith. For Teilhard, the principle of metamorphosis in and through Christ toward final redemption—attaining at last what he termed the omega point—describes the course of spiritual as well as material evolution.[36] And as we have become increasingly aware, such an evolutionary or process theology has considerable bearing on ecological ethics.

The world now finds itself confronted with unprecedented threats of climate change, accelerated extinction of species, overconsumption, depletion of fossil fuels, increasing pollution, and a host of other perils. Responding to such ecological crises demands a fresh version of faith-centered environmental ethics—one that goes beyond the stewardship model of conservation, or even preservation, to seize the prospect of a radical transformation. Envisioning and thereby hastening such a metamorphosis, achieved through the resurrectional triumph of a cosmic Christ, is what rediscovery of a Transfiguration gospel promises for our time. Beauty, joy, and the hope of universal transformation—to all of this the mountain's iconic episode bears witness.

---

34. Teilhard de Chardin, letter of 8 August, 1919, in *Genèse d'une pensée*, 394. (My translation).

35. Callicott, "The New," 166–82.

36. Teilhard's sense of a cosmic Christ, anticipated by Saint Paul, also finds a parallel in the formulations of later ecotheologians, such as Joseph Sittler and Rosemary Radford Ruether. See, for example, Bouma-Prediger's *The Greening of Theology*, esp. 61–101; and Ruether, *Gaia & God*, 229–53.

Postlude: A Sequence of Meditations on Metamorphosis

THOUGH THE TRANSFIGURATION REMAINS a peripheral feature of the church's common liturgical life, it can be more readily accommodated within practices of private devotion. What follows, then, is a suggested daily cycle of reflection on the theme of metamorphosis, a sequence that might be appended to other, more customary forms of prayer and meditation. The sequence, drawn from diverse biblical and extra-biblical sources, with some interpolations of my own, is suitable for individual use or adaptable for group reflection.

Within the week's progression, a particular thematic emphasis is developed for each day. Sunday's accent is on Light, Resurrection, and Creation. The Transfiguration of affliction is highlighted on Friday, while themes of healing, beauty, and Sabbath rest become prominent in Saturday's texts. Though imaged in the gospel episode as achieved within a spot of time, the metamorphosis of humanity, society, and the cosmos—like the course of biological and geological evolution—ordinarily unfolds by slow degrees. So Monday through Thursday follow an evolutionary progression, with the facet of Transfiguration illumined each day, corresponding to a major phase of material and spiritual development. Gustav Mahler's monumental Third Symphony traces a comparable narrative of cosmic metamorphosis: from Creation and the beginning of time, through the formation of the physical universe, the appearance in turn of vegetative and of animal life on earth, and the emergence of humanity leading toward the final consummation of time in God's own time.

Accordingly, Monday's reflections center on inanimate matter and energy; Tuesday's, on vegetative life; Wednesday's, on animate creatures;

and Thursday's, on the metamorphosis of our lives and God's exaltation of human nature.

FIRST WORDS, FOR ANY DAY

Your lightnings lit up the world. (Ps 77:18)

And all of us, with unveiled faces, seeing the glory of the Lord as though reflected in a mirror, are being transformed into the same image from one degree of glory to another; for this comes from the Lord, the Spirit. (2 Cor 3:18)

How lovely is your dwelling place, O Lord. (Ps 84:1)

Rabbi, it is good for us to be here. (Mark 9:5)

Sunday

All praise to you, Transfigured and Transfiguring Lord,
For the life-giving radiance of each dawn;
And for light invisible and uncreated.
Come, Holy Spirit of light and life
Whose breath sustains Creation
And inspires metamorphosis again and to the end, quickened by
    the Resurrection of your Christ.

MAIN SCRIPTURE TEXT

The LORD said to Moses, "Come up to me on the mountain, and wait there; and I will give you the tablets of stone, with the law and the commandment, which I have written for their instruction." So Moses set out with his assistant Joshua, and Moses went up into the mountain of God. To the elders he had said, "Wait here for us, until we come to you again; for Aaron and Hur are with you; whoever has a dispute may go to them."

Then Moses went up on the mountain, and the cloud covered the mountain. The glory of the LORD settled on Mount Sinai, and the cloud covered it for six days; on the seventh day he called to Moses out of the cloud. Now the appearance of the glory of the LORD was like a devouring fire on the top of the mountain in the sight of the people of Israel. Moses entered the cloud, and went up on the mountain. Moses was on the mountain for forty days and forty nights. (Exod 24:12–18)

OTHER EXTRACTS

Then God said, "Let there be light"; and there was light. (Gen 1:3)

Then I saw a new heaven and a new earth; for the first heaven and the first earth had passed away, and the sea was no more. (Rev 21:1)

You never enjoy the world aright, till you see how a sand exhibeth the wisdom and power of God: And prize in everything the service which they do you, by manifesting His glory and goodness to your Soul. . . . You never enjoy the world aright, till the Sea itself floweth in your veins, till you are clothed with the heavens, and crowned with the stars. (Thomas Traherne)

The unity of the world is by nature dynamic or evolutive. . . .
Let creation repeat to itself again today, and tomorrow, and until the end of time, so long as the transformation has not run its full course, the divine saying: "This is my body." (Pierre Teilhard de Chardin)

Blessed are you, Lord, God of all Creation. Through your goodness we have this bread to offer, which earth has given and human hands have made. It will become for us the bread of life.
Blessed are you, Lord, God of all Creation. Through your goodness we have this wine to offer, fruit of the vine and work of human hands. It will become our spiritual drink. (Roman Catholic Eucharistic liturgy)
The Christian hope of the future is that . . . the true message and meaning of the Incarnation will come to be more deeply understood. . . . When this happens, Christian sacramental worship will at last disclose its full meaning and enter into its full heritage. For it will be recognized as the ritual sign of our deepest relation with Reality, and so of the mysterious splendour of our situation and our call: the successive life of man freely offered in oblation, and the abiding life of God in Christ received, not for our own sakes, but in order to achieve that transfiguration of the whole created universe, that shining forth of the splendour of the Holy, in which the aim of worship shall be fulfilled. (Evelyn Underhill)

Hail holy Light, offspring of Heaven first-born,
Or of the Eternal coeternal beam
May I express thee unblamed? Since God is light,
And never but in unapproached light,
Dwelt from eternity, dwelt then in thee,
Bright effluence of bright essence increate.
Or hear'st thou rather pure ethereal stream,
Whose fountain who shall tell? Before the sun,
Before the Heavens thou wert, and at the voice
Of God, as with a mantle didst invest
The rising world of waters dark and deep,
Won from the void and formless infinite. (John Milton)

In the new humanity which is begotten today the Word prolongs
the unending act of his own birth; and by virtue of his immersion
in the word's womb, the great waters of the kingdom of matter
have, without even a ripple, been endued with life. No visible
tremor marks this inexpressible transformation; and yet, mysteriously and in very truth, at the touch of the superstantial Word
the immense host which is the universe is made flesh. Through
your own incarnation, my God, all matter is henceforth incarnate. . . . Now, Lord, through the consecration of the world the
luminosity and fragrance which suffuse the universe take on for
me the lineaments of a body and a face—in you. (Pierre Teilhard
de Chardin)

Monday

All praise to you, Transfigured and Transfiguring Lord,
For clouds, water, iron, and quartz,
Carbon molecules, hydrogen, air, and quarks
For glaciers, lava, cliffs,
And mountain heights,
Sandstone, gold, salt, and iron
For the metamorphosis of earth's crust, star dust, and limestone
For wind, the planets in their orbits, comets, luminous nebulae,
Ultraviolet rays
And all matter, dark and light.

MAIN SCRIPTURE TEXT

Moses came down from Mount Sinai. As he came down from the mountain with the two tablets of the covenant in his hand, Moses did not know that the skin of his face shone because he had been talking with God. When Aaron and all the Israelites saw Moses, the skin of his face was shining, and they were afraid to come near him. But Moses called to them; and Aaron and all the leaders of the congregation returned to him, and Moses spoke with them. Afterward all the Israelites came near, and he gave them in commandment all that the LORD had spoken with him on Mount Sinai. When Moses had finished speaking with them, he put a veil on his face; but whenever Moses went in before the Lord to speak with him, he would take the veil off, until he came out; and when he came out, and told the Israelites what he had been commanded, the Israelites would see the face of Moses, that the skin of his face was shining; and Moses would put the veil on his face again, until he went in to speak with him. (Exod 34:29–35)

OTHER EXTRACTS

Then God said, "Let there be light"; and there was light. (Gen 1:3)

Blessed be you, harsh matter, barren soil, stubborn rock. . . .
Blessed be you, perilous matter, violent sea, untamable passion. . . .
I have no desire, I have no ability, to proclaim anything except
   the innumerable prolongations of your incarnate Being in the
   world of matter. (Pierre Teilhard de Chardin)

The shore is an ancient world, for as long as there has been an earth and sea there has been this place of the meeting of land and water. Yet it is a world that keeps alive the sense of continuing creation and of the relentless drive of life. (Rachel Carson)

Tuesday

All praise to you, Transfigured and Transfiguring Lord, for green
   life on earth:
For flowering myrtle,
Dogwood, algae, broccoli, and wheat,
Sunlight on the ash tree, sycamore, pine, hemlock,
Ancient oak
And Alpine roses on the heights.

MAIN SCRIPTURE TEXT

> Thus says the Lord God: I myself will take a sprig from the lofty top of a cedar; I will set it out. I will break off a tender one from the topmost of its young twigs; I myself will plant it on a high and lofty mountain. On the mountain height of Israel I will plant it, in order that it may produce boughs and bear fruit, and become a noble cedar. Under it every kind of bird will live; in the shade of its branches will nest winged creatures of every kind. All the trees of the field shall know that I am the LORD. (Ezek 17:22–24)

OTHER EXTRACTS

> Let the field be joyful and all that is therein.
> Then shall all the trees of the wood shout for joy
> Before the Lord when he comes,
> When he comes to judge the earth. (Ps 96:11–13)

> Consider the lilies of the field, how they grow: they neither toil nor spin, yet I tell you, even Solomon in all his glory was not clothed like one of these. (Matt 6:28–29)

> Then I was standing on the highest mountain of them all. And round about beneath me was the whole hoop of the world. And while I stood there I saw more than I can tell and I understood more than I saw; for I was seeing in a sacred manner the shapes of all things in the spirit, and the shape of all shapes as they must live together like one being. And I saw that the sacred hoop of my people was one of many hoops that made one circle, wide as daylight and as starlight, and in the center grew one mighty flowering tree to shelter all the children of one mother and one father. And I saw that it was holy. (Black Elk)

> I go among trees and sit still. (Wendell Berry)

Wednesday

All praise to you, Transfigured and Transfiguring God, for our
    brute neighbors on this earth:
For snails, elephants, and sperm whales,
Wolves, tigers, and chimpanzees,
For cattle, cats, horses, and oxen,
Cardinals, wood thrush, sparrows, eagles, and mourning doves
For the metamorphosis of butterflies, grasshoppers, and frogs
For two-legged, four-legged, and crawling creatures
That creep, run, swim, climb, and fly.

MAIN SCRIPTURE TEXT

Can you hunt the prey for the lion, or satisfy the appetite of the young lions, when they crouch in their dens, or lie in wait in their covert? Who provides for the raven its prey, when its young ones cry to God, and wander about for lack of food? . . . Is it by your wisdom that the hawk soars, and spreads its wings toward the south? Is it at your command that the eagle mounts up and makes its nest on high? . . . Can you draw out Leviathan with a fishhook, or press down its tongue with a cord? . . . I will not keep silence concerning its limbs, or its mighty strength, or its splendid frame. . . . It makes the sea boil like a pot; it makes the sea like a pot of ointment. It leaves a shining wake behind it; one would think the deep to be white-haired. On earth it has no equal, a creature without fear. It surveys everything that is lofty; it is king over all that is proud. (Job 38:39–41; 40:26–27; 41:1, 12, 31–34)

OTHER EXTRACTS

I think I could turn and live with animals, they are so placid and Self-contain'd,
I stand and look at them long and long. (Walt Whitman)

It was on that evening that I went on a walk for the first time among the tundra birds. They all build their nests on the ground, so their vulnerability is extreme. I gazed down at a single horned lark no bigger than my first. She stared back resolute as iron. . . . I took to bowing on these evening walks. I would bow slightly with my hands in my pockets, toward the birds and the evidence of life in their nests—because of their fecundity, unexpected in this remote region, and because of the serene arctic light that came down over the land like breath, like breathing. (Barry Lopez)

The water falls of the Sierra are frequented by only one bird,—the Ouzel or Water Thrush. . . . The Ouzel sings on through all the seasons and every kind of storm . . . [with] irrepressible gladness . . . In a general way his music is that of the streams refined and spiritualized. . . .

Why should man value himself as more than a small part of the one great unit of creation? And what creature of all that the Lord has taken the pains to make is not essential to the completeness of that unit—the cosmos? The universe would be incomplete without man; but it would also be incomplete without the smallest transmicroscopic creature that dwells beyond our conceitful eyes and knowledge. From the dust of the earth, from the common elementary fund, the Creator has made Homo sapiens. From the same material he has made every other creature, however noxious and insignificant to us. They are earth-born companions and our fellow mortals. (John Muir)

He will feed his flock like a shepherd; he will gather the lambs in his arms, and carry them in his bosom, and gently lead the mother sheep. (Isa 40:11)

Thursday

All praise to you, Transfigured and Transfiguring Lord,
Who graciously fashioned human beings in your own image,
Granting them understanding, memory, and consciousness,
Will, imagination, and desire,
Implanting in them capacities for love, play, learning, laughter,
　　work, worship, and desire for you.
All praise and thanks for calling these your creatures to become
　　co-creators, heirs of the promise, Sons and daughters of
　　God.

Main Scripture Reading

When they had crossed, Elijah said to Elisha, "Tell me what I may do for you, before I am taken from you." Elisha said, "Please let me inherit a double share of your spirit." He responded, "You have asked a hard thing; yet, if you see me as I am being taken from you, it will be granted you; if not, it will not." As they continued walking and talking, a chariot of fire and horses of fire separated the two of them, and Elijah ascended in a whirlwind into heaven. Elisha kept watching and crying out, "Father, father! The chariots of Israel and its horsemen!" But when he could no longer see him, he grasped his own clothes and tore them in two pieces.

He picked up the mantle of Elijah that had fallen from him, and went back and stood on the bank of the Jordan. He took the mantle of Elijah that had fallen from him, and struck the water, saying, "Where is the LORD, the God of Elijah?" When he had struck the water, the water was parted to the one side and to the other, and Elisha went over. (2 Kgs 2:9–14)

EXTRACTS

What is man that you should be mindful of him?
The son of man that you should seek him out?
You have made him but little lower than the angels;
You adorn him with glory and honor. (Ps 8:4–6)

For he received honor and glory from God the Father when that
voice was conveyed to him by the Majestic Glory, saying, "This is
my Son, my Beloved, with whom I am well pleased." We ourselves
heard this voice come from heaven while we were with him on
the holy mountain. (2 Pet 1:17–18)

The Logos of God became human, that you might learn how a
human may become God. (Clement of Alexandria)

To live the cosmic life is to live dominated by the consciousness
that one is an atom in the body of the mystical and cosmic Christ.
(Pierre Teilhard de Chardin)

We are to be changed. Unless we believe that, is there any point
in our lives? We cannot change other people, one of the hard-
est lessons of all, but we can change ourselves. Everything in the
[Benedictine] Rule, as in the gospel, points to the risen Christ, to
the paschal mystery, to the mystery of death and new life. . . . As
monastics have always known, the most powerful factor at work
upon us, acting to make change, transformation, possible, is the
Word of God . . . Transformation comes about when we are willing to admit God's word into our lives, to hear God's voice and to
act upon it. (Esther de Waal)

Friday

All praise to you, Transfigured and Transfiguring Lord,
Who has borne all grief on the cross
Re-creating your creation;
Who endured torture, death, and rejection,
Blessed One pierced, still pierced, whose wounds remain though
    framed in glory,
Have Mercy.
Stay and stand with those who are sick or lonely, despondent or
    bereaved,
With those imprisoned, disabled, unemployed, and misunder-
    stood,
With those approaching the hour of their death, and fearing
    death.
With all afflicted creatures.

MAIN SCRIPTURE TEXT

See, my servant shall prosper; he shall be exalted and lifted up, and shall be very high. Just as there were many who were astonished at him—so marred was his appearance, beyond human semblance, and his form beyond that of mortals—so shall he startle many nations; kings shall shut their mouths because of him; for that which had not been told them they shall see, and that which they had not heard they shall contemplate. . . . Surely he has borne our infirmities and carried our diseases; yet we accounted him stricken, struck down by God, and afflicted. But he was wounded for our transgressions, crushed for our iniquities; upon him was the punishment that made us whole, and by his bruises we are healed. (Isa 52:13–15, 53: 4–5)

OTHER EXTRACTS

Listen, I will tell you a mystery! We will not all die, but we all will be changed, in a moment, in the twinkling of an eye, at the last trumpet. (1 Cor 15:51–52)

Very truly, I tell you, unless a grain of wheat falls into the earth and dies, it remains just a single grain; but if it dies, it bears much fruit. . . .
"Now my soul is troubled. And what should I say—Father, save me from this hour?" No, it is for this reason that I have come to this hour. "Father, glorify your name." Then a voice came from heaven, "I have glorified it, and I will glorify it again." . . . "And I, when I am lifted up from the earth, will draw all people to myself." (John 12: 24, 27–28, 32)

Like an artist who is able to make use of a fault or an impurity in the stone he is sculpting or the bronze he is casting so as to produce more exquisite line or a more beautiful tone, God, without sparing us the partial deaths, nor the final death, which form an essential part of our lives, transfigures them by integrating them in a better plan—*provided we lovingly trust in him.* Not only our unavoidable ills but our faults, even our most deliberate ones, can be embraced in that transformation, provided always we repent of them. . . . God must, in some way or other, make room for himself, hollowing us out and emptying us, if he is finally to penetrate into us. And in order to assimilate us in him, he must break the molecules of our being so as to re-cast and re-model us. The function of death is to provide the necessary entrance into our inmost selves. (Pierre Teilhard de Chardin)

And al cretures that might suffre payne suffrid with Hym.... The firmament, the erth, faledyn for sorow in hyr kynde in the tyme of Crists deyng. (Julian of Norwich)

Saturday

All praise to you, Transfigured and Transfiguring God, for
Healers and gifts of restoration,
For physicians, nurses, medicines, and herbs,
Hospitals and wise counselors,
for sleep, silence, springs of renewal,
sources of changelessness amid change
and times of Sabbath rest.
In your will is our peace.

MAIN SCRIPTURE TEXT

Now about eight days after these sayings Jesus took with him Peter and John and James, and went up on the mountain to pray. And while he was praying, the appearance of his face changed, and his clothes became dazzling white. Suddenly they saw two men, Moses and Elijah, talking to him. They appeared in glory and were speaking of his departure, which he was about to accomplish at Jerusalem. Now Peter and his companions were weighed down with sleep; but since they had stayed awake, they saw his glory and the two men who stood with him. Just as they were leaving him, Peter said to Jesus, "Master, it is good for us to be here; let us make three dwellings, one for you, one for Moses, and one for Elijah"—not knowing what he said. While he was saying this, a cloud came and overshadowed them; and they were terrified as they entered the cloud. Then from the cloud came a voice that said, "This is my Son, my Chosen; listen to him!" When the voice had spoken, Jesus was found alone. And they kept silent and in those days told no one any of the things they had seen. (Luke 9:28–36)

OTHER EXTRACTS

"Then the angel showed me the river of the water of life, bright as crystal, flowing from the throne of God and of the Lamb through the middle of the street of the city. On either side of the river is the tree of life with its twelve kinds of fruit, producing its fruit each month; and the leaves of the tree are for the healing of the nations." (Rev 22:1–2)

While he was still speaking, suddenly a bright cloud overshadowed them, and from the cloud a voice said, "This is my Son, the Beloved; with him I am well pleased; listen to him!" When the disciples heard this, they fell to the ground and were overcome by fear. But Jesus came and touched them, saying, "Get up and do not be afraid." (Matt 17:5–8)

Worship the LORD in the beauty of holiness;
Let the whole earth tremble before him. (Ps 96:9)

One thing have I asked of the LORD;
One thing I seek;
That I may dwell in the house of the LORD all the days
Of my life;
To behold the fair beauty of the LORD
And to seek him in his temple. (Ps 27:4–6)

How do we know, but the world is that body, which the Deity hath assumed to manifest His Beauty and by which He maketh Himself as visible, as it is possible He should? (Thomas Traherne)

The beauty of the world is the co-operation of divine wisdom in creation. "Zeus made all things," says an Orphic line, "and Bacchus perfected them." This perfecting is the creation of beauty; God created the universe, and his Son, our first-born brother, created the beauty of it for us. The beauty of the world is Christ's tender smile for us coming through matter. He is really present in the universal beauty. The love of this beauty proceeds from God dwelling in our souls and goes out to God present in the universe. It also is like a sacrament. (Simone Weil)

O God, who on the holy mount revealed to chosen witnesses your well-beloved song, wonderfully transfigured, in raiment white and glistening: Mercifully grant that we, being delivered from the disquietude of this world, may by faith behold the King in his beauty; who with you, O Father, and you, O Holy Spirit, lives and reigns, one God, for ever and ever. Amen. (*U.S. Book of Common Prayer*, 1979)

Appendix

Sermon Preached in the University Chapel, Sewanee, 1911, On the Feast of the Transfiguration* by William Porcher DuBose

"I determined not to know anything among you save Jesus Christ, and Him crucified."

—1 COR 2: 2

O N THIS ONE OCCASION of my life, in this place, and upon this spot, I may presume to be somewhat personal. When the suggestion was made to me of this week, naturally the meaning and the possibly useful purpose of it came very powerfully over me, and long and very serious thought arose—of myself, of Sewanee and my forty years here, of the Church that placed us here, of the time, and the times, past and future. What have we done? What are we? What are we going to do and to be? In fact, the very first hint, some years ago, of such an occasion as this came to me coupled with some such questioning: What can we put, not only into shape, but into motion here at Sewanee, for Sewanee, for the Church, for our country and our time? No doubt such questions have come to many of us in the form: What new thing can we devise, what new interest arouse, what new movement inaugurate? I suggest in anticipation what is probably a better form of the query: How can we acquire the secret of making the old ever new, and keeping it so?

* This sermon is reprinted from "Chapter VI, Sermon at Sewanee," in William Porcher DuBose's *Turning Points in My Life* (New York: Longmans, Green and Co., 1912).

Some illustrations have recently come to us right here of how something like that might be accomplished. It is not so long since doubts and fears and forebodings were rife in many of our minds. Under the look of things as they were, it was impossible to come here or be here and not ask: Are we in the right place? How much longer can we live under these conditions? We came here this summer—and looked around—and rubbed our eyes—and asked ourselves: Where are we? What has happened? The old place, the very, dear, old spot, had been transfigured, had become new. With it the whole tone of things was altered: What a beautiful place was Sewanee! What a perfect, predestined spot for such a mind and heart and life centre! But that was not half the transformation. We had heard that students, trustees, alumni, residents were all disheartened and despondent—and, lo! the transfiguration on our mountain top of the mere ground was as nothing to that which had come over the spirit of Sewanee; never was determination so determined, and, by sheer consequence, never were hopes more high or was life more active.

What is the moral already? We do not forever want new things; we want the art of keeping things forever new. The change we need is not in the things, it is in us and our hold upon the things—our life in them, our use of them, our labor for them. Let us remember that our Lord taught absolutely nothing new—the Gospel was older than the Law, God's love than man's obedience. He Himself, the incarnation of our faith, our hope, our life, was before Moses, before Abraham, before Adam, before the foundation of the earth, as old as God, because He was God's love-disposition, love-purpose, Self-realization in us and in His world. Our Lord spoke only of God and of man, and their mutual relations; on God's part, of love, grace, and fellowship or oneness with us (coming down)—and on our part (going up) of faith, hope, and love that make us one with Him. Our Lord uttered no new word, gave no new commandment, even instituted no new sacrament—water and bread and wine were already in themselves not only symbols or signs, but instruments and agents of birth and life. He took all the old things as they were, and He made them all living and new. When He took His disciples up with Him into the very high mountain, it was not really in Himself, but only to them that He was transfigured. They saw Him as the sun and His raiment as the light; they heard words from heaven, claiming Him for God and declaring Him to man. But their so seeing and hearing was only through the exaltation of their own spiritual selves and faculties. Jesus was always so, if their senses could but have perceived it. We do indeed live only in our supreme moments. Things are monotonous, dull, dead enough, day after day, perhaps year after year, until somehow we are taken up—let me say, however, that we are never taken up, except as also, with all our spiritual cooperation, we take ourselves up—into the exceeding high mountain, and there all our world becomes transfigured before us. "Old things are passed away: behold all things are become new." Mind, not all new things have become, or come to pass, but all things, the old things, have become new. God and heaven are everywhere and always here if we could but see them; but alas! almost nowhere, and so seldom here, because so few of us can see them, and we so seldom.

How is it that our Lord Himself could live so continuously and so high? I am speaking of Him humanly; and speaking so, we must remember, however, that He had His deep places as well as His high, His darkness as well as light, His desertions and emptiness as well as His exaltations and fulness, His descents into hell as well as His ascents into heaven. But still, how could our Lord walk as continuously as He did upon the mountain tops, with such deep waters and desert places, such Gethsemanes and Calvaries always beneath His feet? We must look for very old and simple and human answers if we would know our Lord as He came to be, and was, the Way, the Truth, and the Life for us. It is because, what time He could spare from the valleys, ministering to the multitudes, going about doing good, He was wont to spend upon the mountains, drawing breath and strength and life from God.

Let me then state, or restate, my proposition and afterward draw from it one or more corollaries. The proposition is that we do not want any new outward truth or law or scheme in itself, but only a new, and ever new, inward relation, or relation of ourselves to the ever-old, ever-new truth. We want the spiritual art and science of a self-renewing and self-sustaining faith and hope and love. The Jesus who was transfigured upon the Mount is He who is the same yesterday, and today, and forever. The subject of conference in the Transfiguration was the old story of the Cross. They spake of His decease which He should accomplish at Jerusalem. "I determined," says St. Paul, "to know nothing among you save Jesus Christ, and Him crucified." If we cannot get high enough, often enough, to get and keep these truths illuminated and glorified in our minds and hearts and lives, we must be content to remain in the dark. For what is Jesus Christ but God in us and we in God? And what is the

Cross but the actual process by which all that is not God dies in us, and all that is lives and grows in us?, And what other end or content can there be to our faith, hope, and love?

The trouble to which we are ever coming back is that we cannot keep the flame burning more steadily in us, that individuals, communities, churches, the Church of Christ should so live, and so need to live, in mere occasional re-awakenings and revivals. At least, it is a blessing and a comfort to us to know that it is only our own infirmity that it is so; it is something to have discovered, and to be able to hold fast to the discovery, that when we are at our best, and just in proportion as we are at our best, we know the truth and know it to be the truth; and equally, that when we are in the truth, and in proportion as we are so, it gives us all the promised power to be at our best. The power of the truth in that sense to "make us free" is its divine credential to us. We are very finite beings, entrusted with and handling infinite forces. The omnipotence of God is at our puny disposal; His eternal love, His infinite grace, His perfect fellowship and oneness with us are ours to command. "All things are ours" if we will but take them and use them. God does not give piecemeal or half-way; His very kingdom and throne are theirs who will take it; He invites us, in Jesus Christ, to occupy it with Him, and offers as well as bids us to be perfect, even as He is perfect. We have no other end or goal than God Himself. We are very finite beings entrusted with infinite forces; let us not be too much disheartened that they do not work infinitely in us, that we handle them very crudely; we are trying and learning to drive the chariot of the sun. At the same time, let us never cease to aim at and labor for their perfect handling, the straight and true driving. If it be true that we do live, if only in our supreme moments, is not every moment in which we have so lived a new and sufficient proof to us of the eternal and infinite reality of the Life Indeed?—and a new and compelling incentive to us to live it, though it take us forever, and we have to pass through deaths and resurrections, to do so? How much longer and greater a thing is life than we Know or think! In the meantime, the fact that even our Lord, in the needful and inevitable infirmity of our present humanity, had moments in which He needed to know anew that He was the Son of God, that He had to learn afresh upon the very cross that there is no such thing as a divine forsaking, though so often there so seems to be, ought to teach us how to have faith in even our darkest hours, and hope when we are faintest and farthest off.

All the new things, all the modern *isms*, of Christianity that have life in them, as many of them have, are but broken fragments of the Truth that is One and is ever the Same. While our sects and our parties live by the truth that is in them and that is vital in them, they are but too apt to live also in a deadly competition with other truths as true as they, and so in fatal detriment to the whole and the wholeness of truth. The course of truth and of life, with beings such as we are, never can move centrally and evenly, wholly and altogether. It is always one side or some part of it that is in motion or in action, and that too often in a way to incur the misunderstanding and resistance of the other parts. There is always fault on both sides: the new, renewed, or revived side of the truth that is in action is so apt to narrow its outlook and vision to the restricted field of its immediate interest and attention, and then to become exclusive, intolerant, and arrogant toward all other views or conceptions. The side or sides that are not in action, or in the movement, are not as appreciative of, or as hospitable to, the revived truth and life in the new movement as they ought to be—and then they proceed to lower their own life by becoming to the "party" in progress an equally mere party in opposition.

The principle of competition, of antagonistic, divisive, separative, of hateful, hating, and deadly competition, has been prevailing in Christianity just as much as in our earthly life and business. The times are changing, and the call, the appeal, comes to us from every source and direction—comes to us Christians, to show the way, the better way, among ourselves, in our own relations with one another, of love and mutual understanding and peaceful and fruitful cooperation.

We have been here now nearly the week—our week together. I think I have seen everything we have done and heard everything we have said. I have looked and listened with very sensitive and interested and anxious organs, with every sense alert. We who are gathered here are of every sort and of all sorts as to our natural and acquired attitudes toward truth and life; we represent all the sides and aspects of faith and opinion; we have all the allowable differences among ourselves. In all this conference and in all our personal association I have not heard one note, I have not detected one tone that did not, or could not, carry me back behind all our differences to the one theme that has occupied all our thoughts, filled all our hearts, and been upon all our tongues to the exclusion of everything else—The Life—the Life that was lived, that lived, for us—that lives in us, and in which alone we live. In the truest sense we have gone back to Christ, back behind everything else, to Christ, Who is our Life.

We stand indeed today together upon an exceeding high mountain—upon this mountain, not only as itself transfigured, but as itself no less a Mount of Transfiguration. It is our Lord Himself Who has brought us up hither. And we have been talking with Him and with one another about Him. We have seen His face as the sun, and His vesture whiter than any fuller or fuller's soap on earth could whiten it. All our talk has been of Him, of the decease that He accomplished for us at Jerusalem, of the life that He lives with us and in us now and forever.

Bibliography

Alighieri, Dante. *The Comedy of Dante Alighieri the Florentine: Cantica III Paradise (Il Paradiso)*. Translated by Dorothy L. Sayers and Barbara Reynolds. New York: Penguin, 1962.

Alighieri, Dante. *The Divine Comedy of Dante Alighieri: III, Paradiso*. Translated by John D. Sinclair. New York: Oxford University Press, 1961.

Allchin, A. M. "The Sacrifice of Praise and Thanksgiving." In *Profitable Wonders: Aspects of Thomas Traherne*, edited by A. M. Allchin, Anne Ridler, and Julia Smith. Oxford: Amate, 1989.

———. *The World Is a Wedding: Explorations in Christian Spirituality*. 1978. New York: Crossroad, 1982.

Alperovitz, Gar. *The Decision to Use the Atomic Bomb and the Architecture of an American Myth*. New York: Knopf, 1995.

Altman, Nathaniel. *Sacred Trees*. San Francisco: Sierra Club, 1994.

Andreopoulos, Andreas. *Metamorphosis: The Transfiguration in Byzantine Theology and Iconography*. Crestwood, NY: St. Vladimir's Seminary Press, 2005.

Baptism, Eucharist and Ministry. Geneva: World Council of Churches, 1982.

Benz, Arnold. *The Future of the Universe: Chance, Chaos, God?* New York: Continuum, 2000.

Berry, Wendell. "Christianity and the Survival of the World." In *Sex, Economy, Freedom & Community: Eight Essays*. New York: Pantheon, 1992.

———. *A Timbered Choir: The Sabbath Poems 1979–1997*. Washington, DC: Counterpoint, 1998.

Black Elk, Nicholas. *Black Elk Speaks: Being the Life Story of a Holy Man of the Oglala Sioux, as told through John G. Neihardt*. 1932. Lincoln: University of Nebraska Press, 2000.

Bloom, Anthony. *Living Prayer*. Springfield, IL: Templegate, 1966.

Book of Common Prayer, The. Kingsport, TN: Church Hymnal Corporation, 1976.

Bouma-Prediger, Steven. *The Greening of Theology: The Ecological Models of Rosemary Radford Ruether, Joseph Sittler, and Jürgen Moltmann*. Atlanta: Scholars Press, 1995.

Brooker, Jewel Spears. "Youth and Age in T. S. Eliot's Spiritual Development." *Sewanee Theological Review* 49 (2006) 465–483.

Bryan, Christopher. *A Preface to Mark: Notes on the Gospel in Its Literary and Cultural Settings*. New York: Oxford University Press, 1992.

———. *The Resurrection of the Messiah*. New York: Oxford University Press, forthcoming.

Bulgakov, Sergei. "The Exceeding Glory." In *A Bulgakov Anthology*, edited by James Pain and Nicholas Zernov. Philadelphia: Westminster Press, 1976.

Callicott, J. Baird. "The New New (Buddhist?) Ecology." *Journal for the Study of Religion, Nature and Culture* 2 (June 2008) 166–182.

Carson, Rachel. *The Edge of the Sea.* Boston: Houghton Mifflin, 1998.

Dear, John. *Transfiguration: A Meditation on Transforming Ourselves and Our World.* New York: Random House, 2007.

DeWaal, Esther. *Lost in Wonder: Rediscovering the Spiritual Art of Attentiveness.* Collegeville, MN: Liturgical Press, 2003.

Dillard, Annie. *For the Time Being.* New York: Alfred Knopf, 1999.

———. *Pilgrim at Tinker Creek.* New York: Harper Perennial: 1974, 1999.

Dingle, Christopher. *The Life of Messiaen.* New York: Cambridge University Press, 2007.

Dowell, Graham. *Enjoying the World: The Rediscovery of Thomas Traherne.* Wilton, CT: Morehouse Publishing, 1990.

DuBose, William Porcher. "The Reason of Life" (1911). In *A Dubose Reader,* edited by Donald S. Armentrout. Sewanee, TN: The University of the South, 1984.

———. *Selected Writings.* Edited by Jon Alexander, O.P. Mahwah, NJ: Paulist Press, 1988.

———. *Turning Points in My Life.* New York: Longmans, Green and Co., 1912.

EarthDay Network. Online: http://www.earthday.net/about/.

Eliot, T. S. *The Complete Poems and Plays, 1909–1950.* New York: Harcourt, Brace, 1962.

Emerson, Ralph Waldo. *Selections from Ralph Waldo Emerson.* Edited by Stephen E. Whicher. Cambridge, MA: Houghton Mifflin, 1957.

"The Feast of the Transfiguration of Christ." In *Catholic Encyclopedia.* NY: Encyclopedia Press, 1912, 15:19.

Festal Menaion, The. Translated by Mother Mary and Archimandrite Kallistos Ware. London: Faber and Faber, 1969.

Ffrench-Beytagh, Gonville, with Vera Hodges. *Tree of Glory.* Wilton, CT: Morehouse, 1988.

Gatta, John. *Making Nature Sacred: Literature, Religion, and Environment in America from the Puritans to the Present.* New York: Oxford University Press, 2004.

———. "The Interior Progress of Tolkien's Niggle." *Studia Mystica* 3 (1980) 2–15.

———. "Little Lower than God: The Super-Angelic Anthropology of Edward Taylor." *Harvard Theological Review* 75 (1982) 361–68.

Geyer, Douglas W. *Fear, Anomaly, and Uncertainty in the Gospel of Mark.* Lanham, MD: The Scarecrow Press, 2002.

Gorainov, Irina. *The Message of Saint Seraphim.* Fairacres Pamphlet No. 26. Oxford: Sisters of the Love of God/Fairacres, 1972, 1979.

Gordis, Robert. "Job and Ecology (and the significance of Job 40:15)." *Hebrew Annual Review* 9 (1985) 189–201.

Gottfried, Robert R. *Economics, Ecology, and the Roots of Western Faith: Perspectives from the Garden.* Lanham, MD: Rowman & Littlefield, 1995.

Greene, Brian. *The Elegant Universe: Superstrings, Hidden Dimensions, and the Quest for the Ultimate Theory.* New York: Vintage-Random House, 2003.

Harries, Richard. *Art and the Beauty of God: A Christian Understanding.* London: Mobray, 1993.

Hart, Russell M. *The Icon Through Western Eyes.* Springfield, IL: Templegate, 1991.

Hatchett, Marion J. *Commentary on the American Prayer Book.* New York: Seabury Press, 1981.

Hedrick, Joan D. *Harriet Beecher Stowe: A Life.* New York: Oxford University Press, 1994.

Heil, John Paul. *The Transfiguration of Jesus: Narrative Meaning and Function of Mark 9:2–8, Matt 17:1–8 and Luke 9:28–36.* Rome: Pontificio Istituto Biblico, 2000.

Hersey, John. *Hiroshima.* New York: Bantam, 1946.

Hill, Peter, and Nigel Simeone. *Messiaen.* New Haven, CT: Yale University Press.

Hughes, Robert Davis, III. *Beloved Dust: Tides of the Spirit in the Christian Life.* New York: Continuum, 2008.

Julian of Norwich. The Shewings of Julian of Norwich. ca. 1390. Edited by Georgia Ronan Crampton. Kalamazoo, MI: Medieval Institute Publications, 1994.

King, Ursula. *Spirit of Fire: The Life and Vision of Teilhard de Chardin.* Maryknoll, NY: Orbis, 1996.

Krueger Frederick W., ed. *Transfiguring the World: Orthodox Patriarchs and Hierarchs Articulate a Theology of Creation.* Santa Rosa, CA: The Orthodox Fellowship of the Transfiguration, 2006.

Lane, Belden. *The Solace of Fierce Landscapes: Exploring Desert and Mountain Spirituality.* New York: Oxford University Press, 1998.

Lee, Dorothy. *Transfiguration.* London: Continuum, 2004.

Leopold, Aldo. *A Sand County Almanac: With Other Essays on Conservation from Round River.* 1949. New York: Ballantine Books, 1966.

L'Engle, Madeleine. *Walking on Water: Reflections on Faith and Art.* New York: North Point Press, 1995.

Lewis, C. S. *The Lion, The Witch and the Wardrobe.* 1950. New York: Scholastic, 1995.

———. *Reflections on the Psalms.* New York: Harcourt, Brace and World, 1958.

Lopez, Barry. *Arctic Dreams: Imagination and Desire in a Northern Landscape.* New York: Random House, 1986.

Lossky, Vladimir. *The Mystical Theology of the Eastern Church.* Crestwood, NY: St. Vladimir's Seminary Press, 1976.

Macquarrie, John. "Creation and Environment: The Inaugural Lecture at Oxford University." *The Expository Times* 83 (1971) 4–9. Reprinted as "Creation and Environment." In *Ecology and Religion in History,* edited by David and Eileen Spring. New York: Harper & Row, 1974, 32–47.

Matthiessen, Peter. *The Snow Leopard.* 1978. New York: Penguin, 1987.

McGuckin, John Anthony. *The Transfiguration of Christ in Scripture and Tradition.* Lewiston, NY: Edwin Mellen Press, 1986.

McKibben, Bill. *The Comforting Whirlwind: God, Job, and the Scale of Creation.* Grand Rapids, MI: Eerdmans, 1994.

Merton, Thomas. *Conjectures of a Guilty Bystander.* Garden City, NY: Image-Doubleday, 1968.

———. *Contemplation in a World of Action.* Notre Dame, IN: University of Notre Dame Press, 1998.

Messiaen, Olivier. *La Transfiguration de Notre Seigneur Jésus-Christ.* Remarks in liner notes of the CD recording with Reinbert de Leeuw and the Netherlands Radio Symphony Orchestra. Auvidis Montaigne, 1994.

Milton, John. *Paradise Lost.* In *The Poems of John Milton,* edited by James Holly Hanford. New York: Ronald Press, 1953.

Moltmann, Jürgen. *God in Creation: A New Theology of Creation and the Spirit of God.* San Francisco: HarperCollins, 1991.

Muir, Edwin. *Collected Poems, 1921–1951.* New York: Grove Press, 1957.

———. "The Transfiguration." In *Collected Poems, 1921–1951.* New York: Grove Press, 1957, 174–75.

Muir, John. *My First Summer in the Sierra.* New York: Penguin, 1987.

———. *Nature Writings.* Edited by William Cronon. New York: Library of America, 1997.

Nes, Solrunn. *The Uncreated Light: An Iconographical Study of the Transfiguration in the Eastern Church.* Grand Rapids, MI: Eerdmans, 2007.

Ouspensky, Leonid, and Vladimir Lossky. *The Meaning of Icons.* Crestwood, NY: St. Vladimir's Seminary Press, 1982.

Palmer, Parker. *Let Your Life Speak: Listening for the Voice of Vocation.* San Francisco: Jossey-Bass, 2000.

Paton, Alan. *Cry, The Beloved Country.* New York: Scribner, 1987.

Pusey, Edward Bouverie. "Sermon 87. The Transfiguration of Our Lord the Earnest of the Christian's Glory." In *Plain Sermons, by Contributors to the 'Tracts for the Times.'* Vol. 3. London : J. G. F. & J. Rivington, 1841.

Radford Ruether, Rosemary. *Gaia & God: An Ecofeminist Theology of Earth Healing.* San Francisco: HarperCollins, 1992.

Ramsey, Arthur Michael. *The Glory of God and the Transfiguration of Christ.* London: Longmans, Green and Co., 1949.

Revised Common Lectionary: Episcopal Edition. Wichita, KS: St. Mark's Publishing, 1992.

"Roman Catholic Liturgy of the Eucharist." In the "Order of Mass" based on the *Missale Romanum.* Translated by the International Commission on English in the Liturgy, 1970–1985. Revised, Second Vatican Council. Published by the authority of Pope Paul VI.

Rotter, Andrew J. *Hiroshima: The World's Bomb.* New York: Oxford University Press, 2009.

Servid, Carolyn. "The Right Place for Love." In *A Place on Earth: An Anthology of Nature Writing from Australia and North America,* edited by Mark Tredinnick. Lincoln: University of Nebraska Press, 2003.

Siehen, Herman Josef. "La Transfiguration." In *Dictionnaire de spiritualité ascétique et mystique, doctrine et histoire,* edited by Marcel Viller, S.J., and J. de Guibert, S.J. Paris: G. Beauchesne, 1991, 15:394.

Stanford, Donald, ed. *The Poems of Edward Taylor.* New Haven, CT: Yale University Press, 1960.

Steinberg, Michael. *Choral Masterworks: A Listener's Guide.* New York: Oxford University Press, 2005.

Stevenson, Kenneth. *Rooted in Detachment: Living the Transfiguration.* Kalamazoo, MI: Cistercian Publications, 2007.

Stowe, Harriet Beecher. 1852. *Uncle Tom's Cabin or, Life Among the Lowly.* New York: The Penguin American Library, 1981.

Symme, Brian, and Thomas Berry. *The Universe Story: From the Primordial Flaring Forth to the Ecozoic Era—A Celebration of the Unfolding of the Cosmos.* New York: HarperCollins Publishers, 1992.

Teilhard de Chardin, Pierre. *The Divine Milieu.* New York: Harper and Row, 1960.

———. "The Mass on the World." In *Hymn of the Universe*, 19–37. Translated by Gerald Vann. With an Introduction by N. M. Wildiers. New York: Harper and Row, 1961, 1969.

———. Letter of 8 August, 1919. In *Genèse d'une pensée: Lettres 1914–1919*, edited by Alice Teillard-Chambon and Max-Henri Begoen. Paris: Bernard Grasset, 1961.

Thoreau, Henry David. *Walden*. Edited by Stephen Fender. New York: Oxford University Press, 1997.

Tirosh-Samuelson, Hava. "Judaism and Ecology: Historical Overview." In *The Oxford Handbook of Religion and Ecology*, edited by Roger S. Gottlieb. New York: Oxford University Press, 2006, 26–33.

Tolkien, J. R. R. Introductory Note. "Tree and Leaf: On Fairy Stories." In *The Tolkien Reader*. New York: Ballantine, 1966.

Traherne, Thomas. *Centuries*. 1908. Wilton, CT: Morehouse, 1960.

Underhill, Evelyn. *An Anthology of the Love of God: From the Writings of Evelyn Underhill*. Edited by Lumsden Barkway and Lucy Menzies. Wilton, CT: Morehouse-Barlow, 1976.

———. *The Mystic Way*. New York: E. P. Dutton, 1913.

———. *Practical Mysticism and Abba: Meditations Based on the Lord's Prayer*. Edited by John F. Thornton and Susan B. Varenne. New York: Vintage-Random House, 2003.

Von Balthasar, Hans Urs. *The Glory of the Lord: A Theological Aesthetics*. San Francisco and New York: Ignatius and Crossroad, 1982.

Wallace, Mark I. *Finding God in the Singing River: Christianity, Spirit, Nature*. Minneapolis: Fortress, 2005.

Ware, Kallistos. "Eastern Christendom." In *The Oxford Illustrated History of Christianity*, edited by John McManners. New York: Oxford University Press, 1990.

———. "Safeguarding the Creation for Future Generations." In *Transfiguring the World: Orthodox Patriarchs and Hierarchs Articulate a Theology of Creation*, edited by Frederick W. Krueger. Santa Rosa, CA: The Orthodox Fellowship of the Transfiguration, 2006.

Weil, Simone. *Waiting for God*. New York: Harper & Row, 1951.

Whitman, Walt. *Leaves of Grass*. Edited by Scully Bradley and Harold W. Blodgett. New York: W. W. Norton, 1973.

Williams, Rowan. *The Dwelling of the Light: Praying with Icons of Christ*. 2003. Grand Rapids, MI: Eerdmans, 2004.

Wolfe, Gregory. "Editorial Statement: Transfiguration." *Image: A Journal of the Arts & Religion* 27 (2000) 3–4.

Zander, Valentine. *St. Seraphim of Sarov*. Translated by Sister Gabriel Anne, S.S.C. Crestwood, NY: St. Vladimir's Seminary Press, 1975.

Zinn, Howard. *Postwar America: 1945–1971*. Indianapolis: Bobbs-Merrill, 1973.

Index of Names